Bella Ciao

33 1/3 Global

33 1/3 Global, a series related to but independent from **33 1/3**, takes the format of the original series of short, music-based books and brings the focus to music throughout the world. With initial volumes focusing on Japanese and Brazilian music, the series will also include volumes on the popular music of Australia/Oceania, Europe, Africa, the Middle East, and more.

33 1/3 Japan

Series Editor: Noriko Manabe

Spanning a range of artists and genres—from the 1970s rock of Happy End to technopop band Yellow Magic Orchestra, the Shibuya-kei of Cornelius, classic anime series *Cowboy Bebop,* J-Pop/EDM hybrid Perfume, and vocaloid star Hatsune Miku—**33 1/3 Japan** is a series devoted to in-depth examination of Japanese popular music of the twentieth and twenty-first centuries.

Published Titles:

Supercell's *Supercell* by Keisuke Yamada

Yoko Kanno's *Cowboy Bebop Soundtrack* by Rose Bridges

Perfume's *Game* by Patrick St. Michel

Cornelius's *Fantasma* by Martin Roberts

Joe Hisaishi's *My Neighbor Totoro: Soundtrack* by Kunio Hara

Shonen Knife's *Happy Hour* by Brooke McCorkle

Nenes' *Koza Dabasa* by Henry Johnson

Yuming's *The 14th Moon* by Lasse Lehtonen

Forthcoming Titles:

Yellow Magic Orchestra's *Yellow Magic Orchestra* by Toshiyuki Ohwada

Kohaku utagassen: The Red and White Song Contest by Shelley Brunt

33 1/3 Brazil

Series Editor: Jason Stanyek

Covering the genres of samba, tropicália, rock, hip hop, forró, bossa nova, heavy metal and funk, among others, **33 1/3 Brazil** is a series devoted to in-depth examination of the most important Brazilian albums of the twentieth and twenty-first centuries.

Published Titles:

Caetano Veloso's *A Foreign Sound* by Barbara Browning
Tim Maia's *Tim Maia Racional Vols. 1 &2* by Allen Thayer
João Gilberto and Stan Getz's *Getz/Gilberto* by Brian McCann
Gilberto Gil's *Refazenda* by Marc A. Hertzman
Dona Ivone Lara's *Sorriso Negro* by Mila Burns
Milton Nascimento and Lô Borges's *The Corner Club* by Jonathon Grasse
Racionais MCs' *Sobrevivendo no Inferno* by Derek Pardue
Naná Vasconcelos's *Saudades* by Daniel B. Sharp
Chico Buarque's First *Chico Buarque* by Charles A. Perrone

Forthcoming titles:
Jorge Ben Jor's *África Brasil* by Frederick J. Moehn

33 1/3 Europe
Series Editor: Fabian Holt
Spanning a range of artists and genres, **33 1/3 Europe** offers engaging accounts of popular and culturally significant albums of Continental Europe and the North Atlantic from the twentieth and twenty-first centuries.

Published Titles:
Darkthrone's *A Blaze in the Northern Sky* by Ross Hagen
Ivo Papazov's *Balkanology* by Carol Silverman
Heiner Müller and Heiner Goebbels's *Wolokolamsker Chaussee* by Philip V. Bohlman
Modeselektor's *Happy Birthday!* by Sean Nye
Mercyful Fate's *Don't Break the Oath* by Henrik Marstal
Bea Playa's *I'll Be Your Plaything* by Anna Szemere and András Rónai
Various Artists' *DJs do Guetto* by Richard Elliott
Czesław Niemen's *Niemen Enigmatic* by Ewa Mazierska and Mariusz Gradowski
Massada's *Astaganaga* by Lutgard Mutsaers
Los Rodriguez's *Sin Documentos* by Fernán del Val and Héctor Fouce
Édith Piaf's *Récital 1961* by David Looseley
Nuovo Canzoniere Italiano's *Bella Ciao* by Jacopo Tomatis

33 1/3 Oceania

Series Editors: Jon Stratton (senior editor) and Jon Dale (specializing in books on albums from Aotearoa/New Zealand)

Spanning a range of artists and genres from Australian Indigenous artists to Maori and Pasifika artists, from Aotearoa/New Zealand noise music to Australian rock, and including music from Papua and other Pacific islands, **33 1/3 Oceania** offers exciting accounts of albums that illustrate the wide range of music made in the Oceania region.

Bella Ciao

Jacopo Tomatis

Series Editor: Fabian Holt

BLOOMSBURY ACADEMIC
NEW YORK · LONDON · OXFORD · NEW DELHI · SYDNEY

BLOOMSBURY ACADEMIC
Bloomsbury Publishing Inc
1385 Broadway, New York, NY 10018, USA
50 Bedford Square, London, WC1B 3DP, UK
29 Earlsfort Terrace, Dublin 2, Ireland

BLOOMSBURY, BLOOMSBURY ACADEMIC and the Diana logo are trademarks
of Bloomsbury Publishing Plc

First published in the United States of America 2023

Library of Congress Cataloging-in-Publication Data

Names: Tomatis, Jacopo, 1984- author.
Title: Nuovo Canzoniere Italiano's Bella ciao / Jacopo Tomatis.
Description: [1st.] | New York: Bloomsbury Academic, 2023. | Series: 33
1/3 Europe | Includes bibliographical references and index. | Summary: "An
exploration of Bella Ciao, the LP that kick-started the political folk revival in Italy
in the 1960s"– Provided by publisher.
Identifiers: LCCN 2022024833 (print) | LCCN 2022024834 (ebook) | ISBN
9781501372629 (hardback) | ISBN 9781501372612 (paperback) | ISBN
9781501372636 (epub) | ISBN 9781501372643 (pdf) | ISBN 9781501372650
Subjects: LCSH: Nuovo Canzoniere Italiano (Musical group). Bella ciao. | Bella
ciao (Song) | Political ballads and songs–Italy–History and criticism. | Protest
songs–Italy–History and criticism. | Folk music–Political aspects–Italy–History–
20th century. | Folk music–Social aspects–Italy–History–20th century.
Classification: LCC ML421.N86 T66 2023 (print) | LCC ML421.N86 (ebook) |
DDC 782.42162/51–dc23/eng/20220607
LC record available at https://lccn.loc.gov/2022024833
LC ebook record available at https://lccn.loc.gov/2022024834

ISBN: HB: 978-1-5013-7262-9
PB: 978-1-5013-7261-2
ePDF: 978-1-5013-7264-3
eBook: 978-1-5013-7263-6

Typeset by Deanta Global Publishing Services, Chennai, India
Printed and bound in Great Britain

Series: 33 1/3 Europe

To find out more about our authors and books visit www.bloomsbury.com and
sign up for our newsletters.

Contents

Abbreviations of the Archive Funds

Istituto Ernesto de Martino, Sesto Fiorentino

AVANTI   Fondo Edizioni Avanti! / Edizioni Del Gallo

BOSIO   Fondo Gianni Bosio

GALLO   Fondo Edizioni del Gallo / Edizioni Bella Ciao

IEdM   Fondo Istituto Ernesto de Martino

NCI   Fondo Nuovo Canzoniere Italiano

LEAV—Laboratorio di Etnomusicologia e Antropologia Visuale, Università degli Studi di Milano

LEYDI MI   Fondo Roberto Leydi

Biblioteca di Storia dell'Arte, della Musica e dello Spettacolo, Università degli Studi di Milano

CRIVELLI   Fondo Filippo Crivelli

Swiss National Sound Archive, Lugano

LEYDI CH   Fondo Roberto Leydi

Acknowledgments

I would like to express my gratitude to several friends and colleagues who helped me during the research for this book. Antonio Fanelli and Stefano Arrighetti helped me to find my way around the marvelous archive of the Istituto Ernesto de Martino in Sesto Fiorentino. Antonio also was the first reader of the manuscript, and had provided useful feedbacks during the writing process. Nicola Scaldaferri granted me access to Roberto Leydi's archive fund at the LEAV (Laboratorio di Etnomusicologia e Antropologia Visuale, University of Milan), and Emilio Sala allowed me to consult Filippo Crivelli's fund (conserved at the Biblioteca di Storia dell'Arte, della Musica e dello Spettacolo, University of Milan). The book has also benefited from the comments and suggestions of several people, among them Fabian Holt, Franco Fabbri, Simone Garino, Ignazio Macchiarella, Ilario Meandri, Goffredo Plastino, and Alessandro Sanna. Bridget Pupillo translated the first draft, and offered good advice from a non-Italian perspective.

Finally, my gratitude goes to Alice, for her constant support, and to my parents who, back in the early 1990s, handed me a cassette tape with *Bella Ciao* on it, and sang me "Jolicoeur" as a lullaby. Definitely, not the kind of stuff a child should listen to.

(Courtesy of Istituto Ernesto de Martino (IEdM), author unknown.)

Prologue (in the Form of a Picture)

Hanoi, North Vietnam, December 1966. On the left is Enrico Berlinguer, representing the Italian Communist Party (PCI). On the right, Nguyễn Sinh Cung, otherwise known as Hồ Chí Minh, president of the Democratic Republic of Vietnam. In the midst of the war's escalation, leading to the deployment of roughly half a million Americans in the following year, the PCI delegation is in Asia to support the Vietnamese. In the photo, the future secretary of the largest and most powerful Communist Party in Western Europe appears confident as he presents the elderly head of Northern Vietnam (what language did they speak?) with gifts from his Italian comrades. In his right hand, angled for the camera, he holds a vinyl record: *Bella Ciao* by the Nuovo Canzoniere Italiano, released the previous year. In the background, two figures (the interpreters?) follow along, intrigued.

Prologue in the

Introduction

1 A Song, a Show, a Record

Bella Ciao is the title of (at least) three distinct cultural objects.

A song—"Bella Ciao"—sung by Italian partisan troops in the final days of the war of liberation from fascism. Later, especially from the 1960s onward, it has become the song of freedom *par excellence* for many people all over the world. It has been translated into numerous languages and has appeared in recordings, films and TV series. In Italy, it is the unofficial anthem of the part of the nation that upholds the values of antifascism.

A live show, featuring a selection of *canzoni popolari italiane* (Italian folk songs) by the group Il Nuovo Canzoniere Italiano (NCI; literally, The New Italian Songbook), conceived by ethnomusicologist Roberto Leydi and directed by Filippo Crivelli. *Bella Ciao* debuted in June 1964 at the Festival dei Due Mondi in Spoleto, creating one of the liveliest scandals in the nation's musical history and helping to thrust the folk revival movement into the Italian mainstream.

And the LP from that show, released by the label I Dischi del Sole at the start of the year 1965 (NCI 1965a). Continually reissued in the following decades, the album *Le canzoni di Bella Ciao*—known simply as *Bella Ciao*—has become a true alternative classic of Italian discography, and has profoundly influenced both the world vision and the music of activists, researchers, and musicians even today (Tesi et al. 2015). The album as well as the show feature two different versions of "Bella Ciao" in one of its earliest recordings, destined to become a standard for later versions to come. The history of "Bella Ciao"—the song—is largely independent from that of the show and the record, preceding them by several years and surviving beyond them in unexpected ways. However, its centrality in Italian political culture can only be understood in relation to the work of the NCI and the entire project of *Bella Ciao*—the show and the album—to which its initial success is partly owed.

Bella Ciao collects songs of various origins: recorded in the field from the voices of peasants, laborers, and elderly housewives; fished out of old broadsides; or composed from scratch. There are work songs, protest songs, songs of the laborers and the *mondine* (the rice-pickers of the Po Valley), songs of the First World War, songs for gatherings, love songs, etc. Despite their stylistic variety and origin, these songs are intended to represent "real" Italian folk music, at a time when field research was unveiling a network of musical practices and "traditional" repertoires believed to be lost during the years of the country's sweeping modernization. In the intellectual and left-wing context in which this heritage was rediscovered and brought to light, these voices came to represent an autonomous culture, antagonistic to the dominant class, and the cultural vanguard of the proletarian revolution.

The occurrence of these three objects—the record, the show, and the song "Bella Ciao"—unfolds at a fundamental moment, intersecting different cultural processes and suggesting different perspectives. First, *Bella Ciao* was considered the symbolic founding act of the folk music revival in Italy, by virtue of the unprecedented media exposure surrounding the Spoleto incidents and the controversies that followed (all of which will be recounted in Part I of the book). Yet, despite the cultural importance of the Italian revival movement, it was the protagonists themselves who took almost exclusive charge of the narratives of that period and of *Bella Ciao* (Leydi 1972; Bermani 1997). Only recently have scholars begun to question some accepted "truths" about folk and protest songs, incorporating new critical tools and approaching the subject from the perspectives of cultural anthropology (Fanelli 2017), cultural and political history (Love 2018; 2019), ethnomusicology (Plastino 2016), and popular music studies (Tomatis 2016a; 2016b; 2019).

The history and ideology of the folk revival are intertwined with those of ethnomusicology and cultural anthropology. The theoretical reflections which the NCI carried out in relation to *Bella Ciao*—the development of critical and methodological tools to rationalize orality, the field research, the debate on the boundaries of "real" folk music, the political aspects—constitute a fundamental piece in the evolution of an Italian approach to studying musical traditions: Roberto Leydi, creator of the show, would in the following years become one of the leading voices of Italian ethnomusicology; Alberto Mario Cirese, one of the initiators of a new wave of anthropological studies in Italy (Cirese 1973; Dei 2018), participated in the larger debate surrounding folk music and collaborated with the NCI, as did many other intellectuals and scholars. *Bella Ciao* thus represents an (often cumbersome) aspect of the history of Italian social sciences and (ethno)musicology, with which scholars have only recently begun to reckon (Giannattasio 2011; Sassu 2011; Fanelli 2015; Dei 2018; Guizzi and Meandri 2015; Tomatis 2021).

The political and ideological ramifications of *Bella Ciao*, however, extend far beyond the spheres of research and revival. The narrative proposed and popularized by the NCI, which interprets the *cultura popolare* (people's culture) as antagonistic to the dominant class culture, represents a theory championed by the Italian Left from the postwar period up to the end of the 1970s, the years preceding and following the great mobilization of 1968. This perspective places the NCI at the heart of the story, both in its (sometimes complex) relationship with the institutional parties and with the many currents of the extra-parliamentary Left. However, emphasis on this aspect—supported by the NCI itself (Bermani 1978)— led to a neglect of the industrial dimension of the group's activity. The story of the NCI unfolds as that of a small cultural enterprise, an "agile group experimenting with the role of music and popular culture within political struggle" (Love 2018: 218), schizophrenically divided between the need to adapt to the rules of the market system and their radical opposition to it, between the fight against capitalism and the need to submit to its rules; between the distrust of sound media as corruptors of folk authenticity and their exaltation as an instrument of class emancipation. Much of the NCI's activity, through the label I Dischi del Sole, concerns the production of records dedicated to folk revival and newly composed political songs, and the diffusion of field recordings featuring the "real" voices of the people. Despite the centrality which this discography has had in Italian left-wing culture, a reflection on the consequences of the introduction of "folk" and antagonistic music into the mass market has been almost completely lacking in those same contexts (Fanelli 2017: 51). On balance, what remains in the collective memory concerning the NCI and *Bella Ciao* is above all the circulation of recordings, bought and sold, exchanged and copied, listened to collectively or privately, imitated by amateur guitarists and choirs in concerts, sung at demonstrations and political events (or, even, as seen in the opening photo, gifted to famous Vietnamese political leaders). The consciousness of what "folk music" is and what "protest songs" are, and the peculiar overlap between these two concepts in Italy, is often based on "products" of the NCI. The same untranslatability in other languages of the concept of *popolare*, as it is understood in Italy, is a consequence of these circumstances: it comprises the Anglo-American concepts of "folk" and "popular," with predictable difficulties and misunderstandings that, in part, continue even today (Tomatis 2021). To reconstruct the preparation, the production, the reception of the show *Bella Ciao* and its transformation into an album—which is the goal of this book—thus proves to be an excellent means for reflecting on the ambitions of cultural musicology, and for testing the boundaries and validity of many of the categories we still use today to organize our understanding of music.

2 Popular Music and Politics in the "Boom" Years

The Italian political scene after the Second World War was characterized by the central presence of the Partito Comunista Italiano (PCI), the second largest party by consensus in Italy and the most authoritative Communist Party on this side of the Iron Curtain. The country's government, however, was held by centrist parties supported by the United States, and in particular by the Democrazia Cristiana (DC, Christian Democrats), the Catholic party that won the first democratic elections in 1948. The transition from dictatorship to democracy took place under the aegis of a profound continuity of the media system. The Italian public service radio (EIAR) had been broadcasting throughout the national territory as a monopoly since the end of the 1920s. After changing its name to RAI and coming under the control of the DC, in the postwar period the institution continued its activity without substantial changes. Within the framework of the fascist regime's nationalist and propaganda policies, the EIAR had opposed the importation of foreign music and had promoted "Italian songs" of a conservative slant, albeit cosmopolitan in taste, and oriented toward pure escapism. The new RAI would continue along the same lines with the launch in 1951 of the Sanremo Festival, still the most popular musical event in Italy today (Tomatis 2019: 50).

The years leading up to *Bella Ciao*—and in particular the years between 1958 and 1964—coincide with Italy's so-called "economic miracle." Industrial production took off. Large masses of workers migrated to find work in factories, leaving the countryside for the new suburbs of the northern cities. While renouncing "traditional" ways of life and leaving behind their former peasant culture, this new proletariat had access to unprecedented affluence and new consumer goods: cars, televisions, and household appliances, but also vinyl records, the turntable, and the jukebox. It is precisely around these technologies that a revolution in listening practices took place, and music imbued with the American imaginary could finally flourish in the heart of the nascent youth culture.

In addition to rock'n'roll, the new sound media offered fertile soil for the development of other kinds of music, those with artistic or even political ambitions. In 1958, Domenico Modugno triumphed at the Sanremo Festival with "Nel blu dipinto di blu" ("Volare"), an anti-traditional song that helped bring a new generation of singers and songwriters to prominence. Starting in 1960, they would assume the name of *cantautori* (singer-songwriters), representing from that moment on the "artistic" and "poetic" subset of Italian song culture (Tomatis 2014).

The crucial year of 1958 also saw the official formation of the Cantacronache in Turin, Italy's first experiment with songs professing didactic and political intentions (Pestelli 2014; Tomatis 2019: 240–52). The group—which included personalities such as Sergio Liberovici, Fausto Amodei, and

Michele Straniero—was a gathering place for writers and poets such as Italo Calvino and Franco Fortini. For the first time, intellectuals took up the task of songwriting, a practice previously of little interest to the educated classes, who for the most part branded what they called *musica di consumo* (mass consumption music) a low form, far too compromised by the market and popular taste to be worthy of attention. The composition of new songs went hand in hand with an interest in the so-called *canto sociale* (social song): the Cantacronache promoted the revival of the political repertoire of the Resistance, of the First World War, and of earlier social struggles. Neorealism, which had dominated Italian cinema and literature in the immediate postwar years, and which was now in decline, reemerged in popular music, helping to redefine its ambitions and aesthetics (Tomatis 2019: 236–40). If songs were not previously conceivable as a space for dissent, now they could act as a form of political communication; they could narrate the world as it was, and help to change it. From a certain leftist perspective, a "good" song became one that said important things, that conveyed content; one that was "real," "authentic."

The Cantacronache, and more generally the leftist culture of the boom years, adopted the lexicon (and prejudices) of the Frankfurt school, and of Adorno in particular. A few months before *Bella Ciao*, at the beginning of 1964, Michele Straniero— who would later be one of the show's main performers— together with three other members of the recently dissolved group published the first essay on popular music in Italy, *Le canzoni della cattiva coscienza* (The songs of the bad conscience) (Straniero et al. 1964). It is a harsh text, even more

Adornian than Adorno himself. In its deep contempt for mass culture, any space for dissent must be constructed in radical opposition to any compromise with the market (or with "capitalism"). However, it is easily noted (and this is an aspect on which Italian leftist culture has rarely reflected) that the very possibility of producing dissent through songs, records, and books is linked to the instruments of that same mass culture: it is the fragmentation of the public made possible by the rupture of the radio's listening monopoly with the ever-expanding record market, which opens spaces for a left-wing public and its alternative and more distinctive consumption. Included among these new interests, starting in the early 1960s, are the folk revival and protest songs.

3 Communism, Ethnomusicology, and Folk Revival

In a nation characterized by an enormous variety of languages and dialects, where a large part of the population did not learn standard Italian as their mother tongue, the mass media played a key role in the process of nation building. During the fascist rule, the radio, along with the language itself, imposed a style of songs and a way of singing them, to the detriment of the diversity of music within the oral tradition. Traditional music, when considered at all, was often presented in a picturesque manner, offering an idealized vision of local folklore. At the same time, due to ideological biases and delays in technological progress, only since 1948—with the foundation of the Centro Nazionale di Studi di Musica Popolare (CNSMP)—have studies on musical traditions in Italy incorporated aural material and overcome the old idealistic or pseudo-romantic approaches to "folk poetry" (Sassu 2011: 50, 55). It is a shift that involves the radio itself, which opens up spaces for diverse local traditions and allows listeners to "imagine" *another* Italy, with its musical and linguistic differences (Agamennone 2019).

The first systematic field research campaigns in Italy can be traced back to two inspirations. On the one hand, there was a need for "emergency ethnomusicology" to document an oral heritage that seemed destined to disappear rapidly in the years of modernization. On the other hand, the centrality of the "Southern question" came into focus, with special attention dedicated to the depressed areas of the South. The latter was at the heart of the reflection by historian of religion and anthropologist Ernesto de Martino. Working alongside de Martino was ethnomusicologist Diego Carpitella, who in 1954 collaborated with Alan Lomax on the first nationwide recording campaign. Lomax was in Italy collecting materials for the Columbia World Library of Folk and Primitive Music, and later compiled two very influential albums (Lomax and Carpitella 1957a, 1957b), both of which "spoil[ed] still more clichés about sunny Italy," as an American reviewer wrote (Simeone 1959).

The projects of these first Italian researchers reveal scientific and documentary ambitions along with political motivations. Antonio Gramsci's philosophical thought influenced the left-wing intellectual movement during these years, in particular with the publication of his *Prison Notebooks* in 1948. In a few short pages destined to influence the fate of ethnographic research for several generations, Gramsci ([1948] 2011: 186) proposes a new idea of folklore that goes beyond previous naturalistic and essentialist interpretations: it must be understood as a "'conception' of the world of particular social strata which are untouched by modern currents of thought." These strata are the subaltern classes: that is, the social groups on the margins of history, hidden by the dominant culture that erases the historical and political meaning of their thought. Incorporating this new concept of folklore, seemingly antithetical to the earlier romanticized folklore, studies on folk culture evolve from a romantic-nationalist practice of collection to become a science that operates "within the heart of historical-social knowledge and even political practice" (Dei 2018: 23).[1] It is from this starting point that de Martino, in the early 1950s, formalizes the idea of *folklore progressivo* (progressive folklore), a "folklore of the *Resistenza* [the Italian resistance movement against nazism and fascism] and the liberation, of strikes and the occupation of lands and factories" (de Martino 1952). This concept also shares ideas in common with Lomax (1948; Leydi 1972: 30).

It is interesting to compare the Italian path to folk revival with the similar debate taking place in the English-speaking world (Boyes 1993; Harker 1985; Bohlman 1988; Rönstrom 1996; Gelbart 2007; Bithell and Hill 2014; Laing 2014). After the Second World War, new progressive or socialist interpretations replace—or more often coexist problematically with—the older romantic nationalism (Livingston 1999: 75). These conceptions create an implicit equivalence between premodern cultures and contemporary subcultures (Boyes 1993: 13) and tend to place "the folk" outside the bounds of history. The definition of "folk music" proposed by the International Folk Music Council dates back to 1954: folk music is the "product of a musical tradition that has evolved through the process of oral transmission." Indicative of this "folk character" is "the re-fashioning and re-creation of the music by the community" (Gelbart 2007: 2). Folk music therefore not only exists as a remnant of the past but is also defined by "the process of creation." It is thus constructed as "timeless," "shar[ing] much with the idea of 'invented traditions'" (Gelbart 2007: 8, 6).

The ideological originality of the Gramsci–de Martino axis lies instead in the "irruption into history of the subaltern world of the people" (de Martino 1949: 421). The NCI would further develop this perspective in the early 1960s, going beyond the categories of the two thinkers. If one of the most typical elements of any revival is the relationship with the past, primarily in terms of a "fight against modernity" (Rönstrom 1996: 8), the NCI upheld the contemporaneity of folklore against traditionalist interpretations. They took the idea a step further: if folk music is the "real" music of the subaltern classes, it must have political value as such. Folk becomes the expression of an *autonomous* and *antagonist* culture (Leydi 1972: 55).

Socialist-inspired perspectives also contributed to the rethinking of folk in the United States and especially in Great Britain, with its more direct involvement of the Communist Party (Harker 1985: 250; Laing 2014). Yet, the link between Marxist class theory and the musical expression of the people in Italy had a centrality in public debate that was unthinkable in other countries. Throughout the 1960s and 1970s, the PCI was the main organizer of concerts in Italy, thanks to the network of the *Feste dell'Unità*—linked to the Communist Party newspaper, *L'Unità*—where pop stars as well as political and folk singers performed. Particularly after 1968, a myriad of leftist organizations collaborated or competed with the *Feste dell'Unità* network: they released recordings, organized festivals, and offered the folk revival a space to emerge in a sort of "antagonistic mainstream" that represents an Italian peculiarity. Lastly, only in Italy has the folk revival interacted so closely with ethnomusicological investigation, often interpreting the scientific results in a political key (Giannattasio 2011: 75). At the heart of all these events is the "scandal" of *Bella Ciao*.

PART I

The Myth of
Bella Ciao

4 Meet the Nuovo Canzoniere Italiano

The Festival dei Due Mondi (Festival of the Two Worlds), founded and directed by the Italian-American composer Gian Carlo Menotti, is one of the most important theater and music festivals in Italy. The seventh annual edition opened in 1964 with a gala evening dedicated to a new production of Richard Strauss's *Rosenkavalier*, directed by Louis Malle. VIPs—many arriving from the capital, less than two hours away by train—flocked to the Umbrian town in search of a few days of fresh air and authentic atmosphere. Among those spotted by the paparazzi were a veritable catalog of Italy's 1960s elite: the "Lady of La Scala" Wally Toscanini, daughter of the famous conductor; the patron and collector Countess Mimì Pecci-Blunt, granddaughter of Pope Leo XIII; Countess Paolozzi-Spaulding, racecar driver and antiquarian. The actors Raf Vallone, Franca Valeri, Laura Betti, and Thomas Milian, Pia Lindstrom—Ingrid Bergman's daughter—as well as various *mondanume socialisteggiante* (worldly socialist types), as a conservative newspaper wrote (Sanzò 1964). The major national press outlets had their envoys on the spot, in some cases established intellectuals and critics: Ennio Flaiano for *L'Europeo*, Franco Abbiati for *Il Corriere della Sera*, and Giorgio Bocca for *Il Giorno*.

Bella Ciao, at its debut, was viewed as a curiosity. Up to that point, the productions of the Nuovo Canzoniere Italiano had not attracted particular attention. The show dedicated to the Resistance, *Pietà l'è morta* (Pity is dead) which had much in common with the new show in terms of its repertoire, had debuted in April to the complete disinterest of the mainstream media. This reaction was predictable: the members of the NCI were not particularly well known to the public or to insiders, with the partial exception of the director Filippo Crivelli, who in Milan was the well-respected promoter of musical theater in the cabaret style, and the curator of the show, Roberto Leydi.

Born in 1928, Leydi had, from the early 1950s onward, built up a solid reputation in Milan as a journalist and researcher. A jazz enthusiast, he worked as a critic for the socialist newspaper *l'Avanti!*, and was among the first popularizers of American folk music in Italy. In 1954, he published with Edizioni Avanti!—a publishing house linked to the Partito Socialista Italiano (Italian Socialist Party—PSI)—*Ascolta Mr. Bilbo* (Listen, Mr. Bilbo; Leydi and Kezich 1954), a collection of "protest songs of the American people," largely indebted to Lomax's research. In the same year, Leydi also met the American scholar during his research trip around Italy (Ferraro 2015: 75). His background was therefore a peculiar mix of socialism and left-wing Americanism, or the "America of the Roosevelt New Deal . . . of black folk, of the poor in the South, of cowhands in the West, of lumberjacks in the North" (Bermani 2003: 123), whom he had come to know through the recordings of Lomax, Woody Guthrie, and Pete Seeger (Love 2019).

Attempting to adapt that model for an Italian audience, in 1962 Leydi, along with socialist intellectual Gianni Bosio, founded the periodical *Il Nuovo Canzoniere Italiano* as well as the working group of the same name (Leydi 1962). Its activity consisted in coordinating a series of recordings that sought out the voices of day laborers, peasants, and workers. Unlike the research of de Martino and Carpitella, the NCI focused mainly on the Po Valley, the most industrialized area of the country, where political and trade unions of a socialist or communist slant had been rooted since the nineteenth century. Indeed, Bosio and Leydi's project explicitly combined research with political struggle. Above all, it collected examples of the *canto sociale*: social anthems, protest songs, partisan songs, etc. In parallel, the group also promoted the composition of new political songs, collected under the label of *nuova canzone*, as a direct continuation of the activity of the Cantacronache, which in the meantime had dissolved and merged into the NCI (Tomatis 2016a). All these materials were disseminated through stage performances, or among rallies and political gatherings. And, of course, with the help of recordings: in the early 1960s Bosio founded, within the Avanti! publishing group, I Dischi del Sole, destined to remain the primary Italian label dedicated to protest music for the next two decades. On the eve of the Spoleto Festival, I Dischi del Sole had already released twenty-four 7-inch vinyls, moderate successes within the alternative sphere: the sales amounted to approximately 3000 copies a month, of which only a third occurred in record stores, and the rest in cooperatives and cultural circles (Cambria 1964).

The musicians participating in the new production, conceived specifically for the Festival dei Due Mondi, were some of those associated with the NCI project and I Dischi del Sole. They were nearly all non-professionals, in their first appearance on the big stage. Michele Straniero was among the most experienced, thanks to his work with the Cantacronache. Sandra Mantovani, who was also Leydi's wife, had already built a strong reputation as a singer in *Milanin Milanon*, a successful show focused on an urban repertoire in Milanese dialect which Leydi had curated, with Filippo Crivelli as director, in December 1962. Roman musician Giovanna Marini was the only one with classical training: she studied guitar in Rome and Siena with Andrés Segovia, and specialized in lute and medieval music. Along with Marini, Maria Teresa Bulciolu—a student in romance philology—had been singing for some months, specializing in a repertoire of songs from central Italy and Sardinia. Caterina Bueno, hailing from Tuscany, was dedicated to the rediscovery of songs from that area. Silvia Malagugini and Cati Mattea, from Milan, were nicknamed *le bambine* (the little girls) (Malagugini and Mattea 2016: 528): they were eighteen years old and practically making their stage debut. Malagugini was the granddaughter of a prominent socialist parliamentarian. They often attended dinner parties at the Leydi household, along with the guitarist Gaspare De Lama, who came from a jazz background and who was entrusted with the musical accompaniment of almost the entire show.

These city revivalists, however, did not attract the curiosity of the public or the press at Spoleto as the true highlight of *Bella Ciao*. Also featured in the cast were some "authentic" exponents of the folk world: the Gruppo Padano di Piadena and Giovanna Daffini. The first group hailed from Piadena, in the province of Cremona, in the middle of the Padan Plain. A *Lega di cultura* (cultural league) had existed there for some years, an experimental labor association that had established itself as an original "people's university" (Fanelli 2017: 52), with prominent intellectual figures such as Mario and Sergio Lodi and Giuseppe Morandi leading workshops on the pedagogy and culture of the working class. Among the activities of the Lega di cultura di Piadena was the formation of a group of non-professional singers, workers, and masons who specialized in a repertoire of labor, protest, and tavern songs: they were Amedeo Merli, Delio Chittò, and Bruno Fontanella.

Piadena is not far from Gualtieri in the province of Reggio Emilia, the hometown of Giovanna Daffini, by far the most fascinating figure in *Bella Ciao*. Much older than the other participants (in 1964 she was already more than fifty years old; she would pass away just five years later in 1969), Daffini had very different and far more difficult life experiences from those of her colleagues. For many years she had been a *mondina* (rice-picker), but she came from a family of musicians and had always earned a living playing at village festivals and weddings. Although she was presented as an "authentic" and somewhat picturesque character, she was actually the musician with the most live experience of the entire group, albeit on stages very different from those of Spoleto.

5 One Week in Spoleto

The first time most Italians would hear about the Nuovo Canzoniere Italiano, Giovanna Daffini, "Bella Ciao," and the existence of "Italian folk music"—and the fact that it could indeed be political—was on a Monday, June 22, 1964. All the Italian newspapers reported on the riots that accompanied the Sunday premiere of *Bella Ciao* at the Teatro Caio Melisso in Spoleto. Michele Straniero allegedly sang a song deemed offensive to the military—the First World War song "O Gorizia tu sei maledetta" (O Gorizia you are cursed)—and was denounced for his contempt of the armed forces. More generally, as is suggested by some newspapers, the show had divided the audience between Right and Left, between scandalized detractors and enthusiastic supporters.

The primary source for the reconstructions of what occurred is the diary of Giuseppe Morandi ([1965] 2012). A photographer and one of the founders of the Lega di cultura di Piadena, which published his diary in 1965, Morandi kept meticulous track of his impressions and of the events themselves. His narration of the facts can be compared with press reviews[1] and with the accounts provided on numerous occasions after the fact by the protagonists, which often differ in some more or less definitive details. In truth, contradictory elements were already the order of the day in the press reports, fueled by rumors and debates that were immediately politicized.

The press preview was held on Saturday, June 20, and it caused division among journalists, despite having been "weak" (Morandi [1965] 2012: 21). At the end, artistic director Gian Carlo Menotti showed up at the theater to see the video footage,[2] "pale and tormented like one of Bernanos's characters" (Bocca 1964). He had probably not realized the show's potential for controversy, but now someone had put a bug in his ear, telling him that "Bella Ciao" was a communist song (Bocca 1964; Straniero 1965: 63). This was one of the very few references to the song, which was almost never mentioned among the contentious elements of the show. Moreover, in the promotional material of the Festival published in April (and approved by the organization), the show had appeared with the much more neutral title of *Canti e cantastorie italiani* (Italian songs and *cantastorie*).[3]

Some adjustments to the script were requested: one sentence in particular was amended in "La lega" (The league) a protest song from the Po Area: "Crumiri col padrone son tutti da ammazzar" (The scabs with the boss should all be killed) becomes "Crumiri col bastone son tutti da cacciar" (The scabs with sticks should all be chased off). After some thought, Menotti was persuaded not to stop the show (apparently thanks to the intercession of Countess Pecci-Blunt). Some sources suggest that after the preview, the setlist required some corrections and cuts to the second part—the protest and social songs—perceived as "out of tune" and "in bad taste" (Del Re 1964b; Giovannetti 1964). This may very well have occurred: *Bella Ciao* was a work in progress, as the NCI crew only arrived in town on Monday June 15, with just five days available to rehearse.[4]

In any case, unrest and protests were feared and expected. A few days earlier, on June 16, a window of the Messaggerie Musicali record store in Milan, showcasing I Dischi del Sole records, was smashed by unknown persons. Bosio, as evidenced by the many telegrams he sent,[5] attached great importance to the fact. After the preview, Morandi went to the mayor of Spoleto, a communist, asking for support. He was trying to involve some organized groups of activists in view of the debut on Sunday afternoon, for fear of provocations by the fascists.

Sunday arrived. The first part of the premiere ran smoothly. Morandi in his diary barely records the "disapproval" on the face of two "countesses" who are sitting behind him. "We'll see what happens with the second half," was Bosio's comment. "Addio padre e madre addio" (Farewell, father and mother), a song from the First World War sung by the Piadena, caused some murmuring in the hall. This was followed by "Gorizia," which lit the fuse under an already restless segment of the audience. According to the program, Sandra Mantovani was expected to perform the song. Due to the singer losing her voice (at least, this is the official version), Michele Straniero instead appeared on stage. Straniero intoned some verses that were not included in the approved script, probably at the suggestion of Bosio, in direct conflict with the organization's requests (Bermani 1997: 69).

> Traditori signori ufficiali, che la guerra l'avete voluta
> Scannatori di carne venduta e rovina della gioventù.
>
> (Traitors, you officials, sirs, for you wanted war
> Slaughterers of sold meat, and the ruin of youth).

This episode is at the heart of the myth of *Bella Ciao*, and it is therefore necessary to dwell on it. In Morandi's reconstruction, in reaction to these verses, someone shouted "Long live the officers." The protester would later be identified as Francesco Crispolti, a veteran of the Folgore paratroopers who was among the accredited photographers in the theater and who had had the opportunity to attend the preview. A moment of silence followed as the song continued on stage; then someone started shouting "Enough, stop!" (according to the press, it was two journalists: Battistini of the *Giornale d'Italia* and Marzoli of *Il Tempo*, immediately joined by Sandro Morichelli of *La Nazione*, "who lost his father in WWI"; Miranda 1964). The mayor of Spoleto, sitting next to the leader of the PCI and deputy Giancarlo Pajetta, replied with "Get out fascists!" This was followed by "Out, out" shouted at the protesters, who did in fact leave the theater in a group that numbered, based on varying accounts, between twenty and forty individuals.

"Gorizia" was presented in the program notes as "a song of explicit and violent protest against the war, originating on the front during the First World War" (NCI 1964). The song was not exactly a novelty, but one had to have followed the previously marginal activity of the Cantacronache and the NCI to have known about it. It had, in fact, already been recorded by Margot Galante Garrone on an album which Cantacronache had produced four years earlier, in a version collected by Sergio Liberovici in Pomponesco, Mantua, set to a different melody from the one that will be later included on the *Bella Ciao* record but already containing the incriminating verses (Various 1960). The text had already been published several times, and the song had also been performed in another show in Turin.[6] Perhaps significant in this particular incident is the fact that in the Spoleto program notes (NCI 1964), the title was indicated, by mistake, as "O Gorizia tu *sia* maledetta" (O Gorizia *may you be* cursed). The semantic shift is not entirely neutral, especially for those who read the program before hearing the song (as, in fact, the audience would have done at a premiere).

In the setlist, "Gorizia" was followed by "Addio a Lugano" (Farewell, Lugano), an anarchist song well known even to a non-politicized audience; immediately following is "E per la strada gridava i scioperanti" (And in the street strikers sang), a song associated with the 1908 agrarian strikes in Parma, which the NCI had recorded in the voice of Teodolinda Rebuzzi, an elderly peasant woman from the province of Mantua. At this point, again according to Morandi's account, the "countesses" began to shout "Buffoons, buffoons." Giorgio Bocca, who shared box seats with Leydi right over the head of our witness, shouted "Vai fuori, carampana" (Get out, crone) to one of the two women, who replied, "Sta' zitto paesano" (Shut up, hick). Meanwhile, Gianni Bosio stood up, proclaiming "This is History, ma'am," triggering one of the "countesses" to respond with what was destined to become famous in the construction of the myth of *Bella Ciao*: "Io *possiedo* trecentotrenta contadini e nessuno dorme nelle stalle" (I *own* three hundred and thirty peasants, and no one sleeps in the stables).

At the next piece, "Son cieco" (I am blind), the two women left the hall, and the performance ended with applause. In the following days, the newspapers would report similar versions, and one wonders if Morandi might also have drawn on them in his reconstruction, or if, on the contrary, he acted as a source for some of the journalists. According to *l'Avanti!*, for example, the statement by the "countess" was "whispered" and was: "I have three hundred and twenty peasants, but none of them sleeps in the hay." Another spectator commented on a verse from the same song (presumably "nelle stalle più non vogliam morir," [we don't want to die in the stables any more]), saying: "If only they had all died!" (Bertero 1964). In Bocca's (1964) account, the peasants are 10 fewer still, 310, and elsewhere 300 (Cambria 1964).

Putting aside the colorful details and the number of peasants owned, these facts in themselves would not justify a national scandal. Throughout the 1960s and 1970s, political protests at shows were the norm. The Spoleto show, however, was also attended by members of the military, a fact which the NCI would certainly have known, given that the city housed a military academy. One colonel, Piacentini, was seen leaving in tears "from humiliation and offense" (Sanzò 1964); according to other testimonies, he instead cried on his wife's shoulder during "Gorizia" (Morandi [1965] 2021: 33). Shortly after the show ended, rumors began to circulate that Straniero would be denounced and charged. The complainant was a police captain, Alferano. Newspapers spread the news immediately.

Immediately after the show, an emergency meeting was held at Menotti's home, with the representatives of the NCI (Bosio, Leydi, Crivelli), the mayor, and Nanni Ricordi, whom Menotti accused of inviting *Bella Ciao* to Spoleto. In response, Ricordi resigned from his role as secretary of the Festival. The artistic director wanted to stop the show or eliminate all political songs; compromise solutions were proposed: for example, balancing socialist chants with fascist chants. The NCI refused to carry out censorship, consenting only to cease performances of "Gorizia."

It was a choice dictated by caution: the following morning, it turned out that charges had also been extended to Crivelli, to Bosio—as managing director of Edizioni Avanti!—and to Ricordi. As specious as they may seem, charges of contempt against the armed forces were perceived as a very serious matter: many at the time recalled the precedent of the Aristarco-Renzi case, eleven years earlier, when the director of the periodical *Cinema Nuovo*, Guido Aristarco, and the critic Renzo Renzi, landed in prison for publishing the story outline for a film on the Italian occupation in Greece (Love 2018: 248). Straniero, moreover, had already been convicted for slander against the head of a foreign state, the Catholic religion, and for obscene publication, for the Cantacronache's record *Canti della Resistenza spagnola* (Songs of the Spanish Resistance; Various 1961). Thus, he could not hope for a suspended sentence, but instead risked three to twenty-four months in prison.

The organization mulled over a possible cancellation of the show: the first repeat performance was in fact scheduled no earlier than Wednesday, June 24. Meanwhile, as the newspapers gave ample space to the scandal, the events of Spoleto entered the national political debate. The former NATO general Erasmo Graniti, president of the local section of the National Union of Retired Officers of Italy (UNUCI), took action to request a direct intervention by the Minister of Defense, Giulio Andreotti, and had polemical posters attached to the walls of Spoleto. The Army High Command summoned another colonel, Gueli, to Rome to report on the facts; shortly before, Menotti went to the barracks with the President of the Spoleto Tourist Board and offered his official apology. The command prohibited the military from participating in the Festival's performances.

The machine was now in motion, and the first parliamentary questions arrived: two were signed by the liberals, and one by the neo-fascists of the Movimento Sociale Italiano (Italian Social Movement—MSI). The Communists counterattacked a few days later, denouncing to Andreotti "the atmosphere of moral lynching toward the artists" and recalling that *Bella Ciao* was "a re-enactment of true voices taken from folklore" (*L'Unità* 1964). The festival management disowned the show with a press release declaring itself "wholly unconnected to the incident" (Morandi [1965] 2012: 38). The NCI issued an independent press release and sent a telegram to Prime Minister Aldo Moro (of the DC) and (socialist) Vice President Pietro Nenni, asking for "open defense of freedom of expression and historical documentation." Dozens of telegrams of support arrived for the NCI and for Straniero (Morandi [1965] 2012: 48-49). The echo of the scandal also reached the United States (*Daily American* 1964) and the Soviet Russia (Ratushniak 1964). Repeat performances of *Bella Ciao* took place regularly.

Meanwhile, in Spoleto, the rumor spread that teams of fascists were coming, and some newspapers announced the presence of Giorgio Almirante, the controversial leader of the MSI (which was never confirmed). The performance on June 24 went off without incident. The next day, however, the press reported two bomb threats called in by phone. Indeed, at the end of the show, a fake bomb was found near the stage. This circumstance, which Morandi downplayed as an almost comic episode, was widely reported by all the newspapers, performing variations on the theme of "how the fake bomb was made" (an alarm clock, a box or a pack of candy, putty, etc.). Nevertheless, the performance on June 25 also took place with no problems, while there was a bit of apprehension for those on the weekend. The NCI failed in its attempt to bring in organized labor groups from nearby Terni (home to a large steel plant and therefore to a very strong union) as a "defense" in case of clashes: the tickets were too expensive, and it was impossible for workers to return by train after the show. In any case, the various unions were warned in advance and helped to create propaganda.

On Friday evening, with a full house and the theater guarded by police, a group of protesters showed up and began making noise during the song "Porta Romana," which contains some salacious double entendres ("It's immoral!" they shouted); according to some sources, the protesters were waving "small tricolor flags" (*Il Messaggero* 1964). Some of the audience left the theater, fearing clashes. Toilet paper was tossed on stage as the atmosphere in the room heated up. Someone threw a handful of coins in the faces of the Piadena members, who continued singing. At one point a spectator climbed up and tried to get onto the stage, followed by another. He was stopped by the police, while Giovanna Marini had already taken up her guitar like a club, ready to hit him. The lights came on and scuffles followed, until the small group of protesters was thrown out. The show continued to its the conclusion. This was the only other moment of protest in the theater after the premiere, but it received almost no media attention, because the next day the newspapers went on strike (Morandi [1965] 2012: 62). *Bella Ciao* closed with its final performance on Monday, June 29. It would prove to be among the greatest box office successes of the 1964 Festival dei Due Mondi.

6 Constructing the Myth
The Countess, the Colonel, the Rice-Picker

As the founding myth of Italy's folk revival, the Spoleto performances were the subject of endless reworkings by those who were there (and, in truth, also by those who were not there). If, as we have seen, it is sometimes difficult to reconstruct the factual reality of what occurred, at the same time that "reality" seems to be less important than its narratives. It is also necessary to dwell on the ways in which the events have been distorted, the ways in which memory—or opportunity—has modified or corrupted them, which parts have been remembered, which have been forgotten, which have been kept silent.

As with any myth, the Spoleto story as it was told after the facts functions by means of simplification: the structure tends to remain fixed while the details change. The two moments of protest in the theater—the initial episode of "Gorizia" and the attempt to crash the stage on June 26—are merged into a single unit of time, as Straniero does in his 1994 reconstruction of events (Straniero G. and Barletta 2003: 41), and Giovanna

Marini does as well (Marini 2005; Macchiarella 2005: 47). Similarly, the various people who actually played a role in the story are reduced to a few topical characters, who in themselves summarize certain characteristics and who play—as in any myth—different actantial roles, taking on certain agencies that, in reality, concerned altogether different subjects.

The "countess," for example. The idea that the dispute started with a noblewoman is something we learn from Morandi, who speaks generically of two "countesses" (and who could not have meant the term in a literal sense, nor could he be certain of the nobility rank of those seated nearby). And yet, the figure of the "countess" always appears in the tales of Spoleto. She is attributed with one of the statements of disapproval most often cited in the reconstructions, namely: "Io non ho pagato duemila lire per venire qui in teatro a sentire cantare in palcoscenico la mia donna di servizio" (I did not pay two thousand *lire* to come here to the theater and hear my servant sing on stage), allegedly addressed to Giovanna Daffini, whose vocal quality (as we will see below) is actually one of the elements of originality in *Bella Ciao*. The episode is tantalizing, and certainly plausible. However, we find no evidence of it, either in Morandi's diary or in the sources of the time. The main source seems to be Giovanna Marini, who has told it on several occasions, always with variations (Marini 2005: 170; Macchiarella 2005: 47; Marini 2012: 10; Valtorta 2018). A similar anecdote was later noted by Bermani (2020: 39), who speaks of "a jewel-encrusted lady" who shouted: "I did not come to the theater to hear my servant sing." In other accounts, however, the countesses even "fainted" (Gabrielli [1971] 2016: 624). The character of the "countess" (better if bejeweled) therefore serves as an embodiment of the conservative elite, of the dominant culture. The same mechanism would occur a few years later in the most famous Italian song of the 1968 protests, published by I Dischi del Sole: "Contessa," by Paolo Pietrangeli (1968). In the song, an imaginary dialogue is staged between a character who despises the workers and students on strike and who, in the rhetorical fiction, addresses a countess. In fact, Spoleto's society column shows just how many of the "real" countesses present belonged to the progressive elite; they were leftist sympathizers and active supporters of the NCI.

The other recurring antagonist is "the colonel," the protagonist of the minor but symbolically powerful episode of the tears of humiliation. In the subsequent narratives, he becomes both a protester in the theater and the manufacturer of the charges filed against the NCI, and together with the countess he completes the lineup of "enemies" from the ruling classes—nobles and warriors allied against the people.

On the side of good—and allies themselves—are the rice-picker and the researcher. The first is the perfect heroine of the people; the second represents left-wing humanism that seeks to give voice to those people. It is perhaps significant that, in her stories, Giovanna Marini (2005: 170) sometimes attributes the episode of the guitar wielded on stage not to herself, as reported by Morandi ([1965] 2012: 59, 64), but instead to Giovanna Daffini. And at times she has transformed the protester who tries to swarm the stage . . . into a countess (and even into the aforementioned Wally Toscanini, who in reality would have been in favor of the performers; *L'Espresso* 1964). Sometimes, the guitar is even "broken over the head" of the invader by Daffini (whereas Marini would have refrained because "I remembered that it cost 300,000 *lire*"; Valtorta 2018).

Equally interesting is that subsequent reconstructions also give the "workers" a central role, magnifying an episode that appears rather minor in the reports of the time; that is, the attempt to include the Terni steel mill workforce, or some former partisans (Marini 2005: 172), as a sort of "security service" against fascists. Some memories mention the "buses of workers from Terni" organized by "Pajetta to defend our right to sing" (Malagugini and Mattea 2016: 524). In her monologue on "Gorizia" in the anniversary performance of *Bella Ciao*, the singer Lucilla Galeazzi (2015), a long-time collaborator with Giovanna Marini, reported a phone call from Pajetta to the youth division of the PCI in Terni, in which the communist leader demanded in no uncertain terms that they send contingents of workers, who promptly crowded the theater and targeted the fascists in the audience with chairs thrown from the theater boxes. There is no evidence of these events in the sources of the time.

Therefore, in light of the documentary reconstruction of the facts and the construction of the narratives of *Bella Ciao* as folk revival's founding myth, the Spoleto controversies must be problematized and put into perspective, if not partially downplayed. The attention of the press amplified the controversial effect of the show, already transforming it, in the aftermath of the premiere, into a deeply symbolic moment (Love 2018: 243). The NCI itself contributed quite heartily to the process: far from considering the protests as incidental, it attributed a political slant to the story and, through its channels, recirculated the negative reviews and the "distortions" of the right-wing newspapers (Straniero 1965; Morandi [1965] 2012), using them to confirm its own point. *Bella Ciao*, wrote Straniero (1965: 62), was intended "to verify a working hypothesis: whether or not the proposal of folklore [. . .] contains an intrinsic, provocative ('revolutionary'?) potential." "The fascist uproar," wrote Bermani (1964), "gives every impression of having been one part of a more global stance of the most reactionary elements of a certain 'official' culture towards the cultural work" of the NCI, which sought to "emphasize the existence of an autonomous proletarian culture, as an alternative to the type of mass culture which reaction wants to impose." In the aftermath of Spoleto, most of the communist and socialist newspapers echoed the same positions on the disruptive value of *Bella Ciao*, since the members of the group had close ties with the parties' newspapers and magazines and often collaborated with them.

Bella Ciao therefore resembles a self-fulfilling prophecy. The show was conceived as the vanguard of a new, provocative, and radical way of interpreting the relationships between classes. It was the political ambition of the NCI to exploit the potential of the folk music revival, in a cultured and elite environment like Spoleto, in order to rewrite and subvert these relationships. The controversy—which may very well have been sought out intentionally, at least on the part of Bosio—was used to prove the point. *Bella Ciao*, for the left-wing public, offers proof that its basic thesis is valid: folk music is truly provocative, and antagonistic to the dominant culture that would like to conceal and eradicate it. What is now called the "Spoleto scandal" concerns, only at first glance, "the words of a song from the First World War." In reality, it was triggered "by the revealed presence of the world of the people and of the proletariat" (Umberto Eco, quoted in Leydi 1972: 56). Or, at least, this becomes the official narrative from here forward.

7 *Bella Ciao* in the Theater
Protest and Distinction

If the far right and the military were outraged by "Gorizia," effectively playing into the hands of the NCI, most newspapers, even some conservative ones, recognized that the "scandal" was disproportionate, and that the song is actually a historical document. Such was the position, for example, of intellectuals like Ennio Flaiano (1964), as well as that of Catholics, who noted that even the Pope had called the Great War a "useless massacre" (Amadini 1964). A study of the reception of *Bella Ciao* in the wider press indeed provides a far more complex and diverse image than that proposed by the NCI.

Even during the Festival, the NCI described *Bella Ciao* as a foreign body, a moment of radical rupture. The presence of the group in a chic and bourgeois environment could not fail to raise some eyebrows, of course. For example, the conservative weekly *Lo Specchio*—certainly exaggerating for the benefit of its readers—described the appearance of the "members of *Bella Ciao*'s troupe, decked out like Fidel Castro's *barbudos*." And yet, even the most conservative of journalists must admit that, in Spoleto, "we have seen worse" (Sanzò 1964). As alien as characters like Daffini and the Piadena might be, in 1964 the public should not have been surprised by the presence per se of folk songs in a "serious" festival. In 1962, the Festival dei Due Mondi had hosted with great success *Black Nativity*, a show by Langston Hughes based on a repertoire of African American spirituals. Behind the NCI's engagement was the ambition to promote Italy's response to American folk revival, at a time when it was becoming quite popular among urban elites. Even less so could the presence of polemical content *in itself* be considered frightening. The audience of the Festival dei Due Mondi was accustomed to political theater, and controversy and censorship plagued other Spoleto shows, even during the same 1964 festival,[1] although they were assisted by poor media coverage since they did not involve any official charges (or because no one fanned the flames of controversy). As noted in PCI's weekly *Vie Nuove* (1964), if *Bella Ciao* did indeed represent "the most daring entry" in the history of the festival, it "in no way contradicts its typical formula: protest songs are ignored by the official culture just as much as other countercultural works" so dear to the artistic directorship. In *L'Unità*, Leoncarlo Settimelli (1964a) recognized the ongoing cultural accreditation of folk music, comparing its appearance at Spoleto to "that of jazz, in 1938, at Carnegie Hall."

Indeed, *Bella Ciao* came at the peak of folk music's recognition, under way for some time in intellectual circles, particularly in Milan, and beginning to make its way into the general public as well. In July 1964, in the aftermath of Spoleto, a long piece in the *Settimana INCOM* (a weekly magazine tied to the centrist Christian Democrats) described "Milan's latest hobby" as follows:

Nuovo Canzoniere Italiano's *Bella Ciao*

40

You come across a restaurant in Porta Ticinese, and along with the cooked sausage and lentils, you are served a dose of ruffian with a three-day-old beard, frayed jacket, shirt open to show his skinny neck, who, at the back of the semi-dark pergola, accompanying himself on the harmonica, sings the tale of a certain Rusina and her *rocheteé* ("pimp" in Milanese dialect) . . . You start browsing a friend's record collection and you swear you find the album *Canti sociali* by Roberto Leydi . . . Just five or six years ago, all this was the stuff of a small group of initiates. Material for intellectuals with complicated and culturally "engaged" tastes. (Ravaioli 1964)

As Dei has noted (2018: 115), the folk revival emerged during these years as a "distinctive element of a precise socio-cultural group." This "distinction," in the sense which the sociology of Bourdieu (2010) gives to the term, stands in relation to the vulgarity of the lower classes that adhere to the models proposed by the cultural industry. It is compatible with the intellectual class's contempt for mass culture, and offers an alternative to it. In other words, while the "subaltern classes" (often enthusiastically) embraced new consumption and new practices in the boom years—songs from the Sanremo Festival, rock'n'roll, the pop music of the British Invasion and, starting in 1964–65, the folk music of singer-songwriters like Bob Dylan—the urban and bourgeois intellectual elites "distinguished themselves" by recovering what was left behind by "the people."

Indeed, most of the press's criticism against *Bella Ciao* concerned not so much the case of "Gorizia" as the paradox of "songs of the people reserved for an elite crowd" (Del Re 1964a) and the accusation of being what, in contemporary terms, we would call "radical chic." That is, the tendency of a certain cultural milieu to seek "primitivism! The naïve!" as noted for example in *Il Tempo* (Giovannetti 1964), following the "fashion" of "strumming the guitar," "widespread among the high-class girls," the "nice and sophisticated . . . university students" (Griffo 1964). If the NCI flaunted itself as the vanguard of the lower classes, a megaphone for their autonomous and antagonistic voices, much of the criticism interpreted *Bella Ciao* as a bourgeois pastime.

For Franco Abbiati (1964)—music critic for *Il Corriere della Sera*, Italy's largest and historically conservative newspaper—*Bella Ciao* instead evoked "the precise memory of a ramble of yesteryear among the taverns of Romagna" and the "songs of a genuine folk tradition, to be imbibed deliciously in small sips, like a good glass of *albana* wine." Similar analyses are found in several reviews, both from the right and from the left, and mostly positive, which read the show in a romantic-bucolic frame. This "bourgeois approval" caused a crisis for the NCI: "We truly regret that certain newspapers speak well of *Bella Ciao*," noted Morandi in his diary, while the troupe laughed at Abbiati's "inventions" (Morandi [1965] 2012: 39, 29).

As NCI's political battle also played out within the reception of its own cultural project, this way of enjoying *Bella Ciao* and folk music paints a complex picture. Folk is as much a musical genre with antagonistic value as it is a distinctive consumer product of the intellectual classes, radical in its ambition but not free from romantic vestiges in the way in which it emphasizes authenticity and genuineness. While constructing the alterity of "folk music," therefore, *Bella Ciao* helped to affirm its aberrant interpretations (from the perspective of the

NCI), by which folk can be appreciated simply *as music*: as an elite hobby among the urbanite "high-class girls," or for the romantic pleasure of its "authenticity." The story of *Bella Ciao* in Spoleto reveals the political agenda of a group of researchers and left-wing activists, determined to disseminate a new interpretation of what folk music is and what it should do, as well as the fact that in the mid-1960s, folk and protest songs had become part of the distinctive cultural consumption of progressive urban elites. With a paradox which the critic (and in turn revivalist) Leoncarlo Settimelli (1964a) immediately noted in the pages of *L'Unità*:

> But won't it happen … that the rice pickers' songs will be played in parlors while the rice pickers themselves will continue to listen to [popstars like] Celentano, Rita Pavone and Gino Paoli?

8 After Spoleto

The visibility gained in Spoleto immediately paid off. During the second half of 1964, NCI correspondence[1] shows a growing demand for shows. The organization was entrusted to Nanni Ricordi. After a break for the summer, the group began to tour intensely. Yet, the actual show was not performed again until the spring of 1965, with some variations in repertoire and cast: the singer-songwriter Ivan Della Mea was added, while a singer of Israeli origin, Hana Roth, replaced Bulciolu—busy writing her dissertation—in several performances; in the Gruppo Padano di Piadena, Policarpo Lanzi took the place of Delio Chittò. *Bella Ciao* was at the Teatro Regio in Parma for the twentieth anniversary of the Liberation on April 24–25, 1965, then from May 3 to May 23 at the Teatro Odeon in Milan for a total of twenty-two performances, and again at the Teatro Duse in Genoa for eleven performances between May 25 and June 2. On these occasions, tickets were offered at discount prices to activists, and the communist and socialist press mobilized in support. These actions were an attempt to resolve the contradiction that emerged in Spoleto, where tickets were too expensive for working-class laborers (Love 2018: 233).

After the comeback tour, *Bella Ciao* was permanently retired. In fact, already in the days following Spoleto, the NCI showed some doubts about performing it again. Several requests for repeat shows had been rejected, for example at the national *Festa dell'Unità* in Bologna (a very prestigious event). *Bella Ciao* was seen as a project that could only be performed in a theatrical and bourgeois context, and not at a "mass festival."[2] Moreover, its provocative value was considered limited, or already worn thin by scandal. The group chose instead to invest in the show's "twin," *Pietà l'è morta*, which had a very similar cast and shared some songs with *Bella Ciao*, but was more economical, more streamlined in terms of lighting and sets, and—above all—was composed entirely of protest songs.

The opposition between the two shows seems to foretell the divisions within the NCI itself (Love 2018: 264), which would come to a head in 1966 during the production of the show *Ci ragiono e canto* (I think and I sing) directed by Dario Fo. Bosio, who would be the driving force of the NCI until his death in 1971, wanted to promote initiatives that were of an explicitly provocative political nature. Leydi was instead leaning toward a performance that, like *Bella Ciao*, offers a "global representation of the folk world" (1972: 56) with greater attention to philology—although around the same time he did collaborate on "pop" recitals, for example with the singer Milva (one of the reasons for his disputes with the other members of the NCI). He left the group, and in 1967 staged *Sentite buona gente* (Listen, good people), the first show entirely centered not on revivalists but on "authentic" performers, in collaboration with Diego Carpitella (Ferraro 2015). Although the importance of these shows remains fundamental in the subsequent development of the folk revival movement, it is *Bella Ciao* that remains within the collective memory, especially due to the success of the 33 rpm record.

9 *Bella Ciao* on Disc
Antagonism and the Market

At the beginning of 1964, Edizioni Avanti! cut loose from the PSI to become an independent publishing house, not directly linked to any political force and willing to support radical leftist positions not aligned with the established parties (Scotti 2018: 185). Previously, in 1960, Bosio had created I Dischi del Sole within the publishing house. The first title released was a 45 rpm with the recording of a message by the socialist leader Pietro Nenni (1960). In conjunction with the release of the first issues of *Il Nuovo Canzoniere Italiano*, the group's research activity, and in collaboration with Leydi, the production intensified after 1962. The first collections of protest songs were released. It is significant that a small publishing house, which until then had published books featuring the writings of Marx, Engels, Rosa Luxemburg, and the first Italian edition of Ernesto Che Guevara (but also the poems of Nazim Hikmet and *Cipì* by Mario Lodi, a future bestseller of Italian children's literature) decided to produce records as well. The choice should be understood in light of Gianni Bosio's original positions on the political value of oral culture, to which the boom in the record market offered an unprecedented chance at success.

Against the majority of intellectuals, Bosio argued that the oral culture of the proletariat was subordinate to the dominant culture, in part because of the established leftist parties themselves, which favored cultural policies whose objective was to bring high culture to the working classes: this was in fact the goal which communist leader Palmiro Togliatti expressed for PCI (Fanelli 2017: 57). The goal of proletarian revolution, on the contrary, must be reached by valorizing the people's culture as autonomous and antagonistic. Being oral, it cannot be conveyed through writing. The tape recorder can be a tool for its redemption. Bosio would praise this new technology in the form of an essay (titled "Elogio del magnetofono" [In praise of the tape recorder]): "the tape recorder restores to culture, once reliant on means of oral communication, a tool to help it emerge, form consciousness" (Bosio [1967] 1998: 158). This tool, which is at the heart of a project of class emancipation, is at the same time becoming central to the scientific project of ethnomusicology, as it represents the way to "save" the voices and sounds of a rapidly disappearing tradition.

Bosio's choice to focus on the record market represents the extension of this line of thought. The catalog of I Dischi del Sole[1] reads: "We use the record as the book has always been used: as a tool for communication and information. There is a difference: the record communicates to everyone; the book does not." The book is interpreted in a historical and materialist perspective as a medium of transition from a culture reliant on means of oral communication to "Culture" as an expression of the ruling class; the record is instead a democratic instrument, because it speaks to everyone.

It is therefore quite predictable that *Bella Ciao* would make its way onto vinyl. The recording of *Le canzoni di Bella Ciao*—I Dischi del Sole's first LP—was organized for November 1964.

After a postponement due to the difficulty of gathering all the performers together, the recording session would take place between the end of the month and the beginning of December, "in a single day, at minimum cost" (Deichmann 2016: 559). The performers received 20,000 lire each (except for the three members of the Piadena, who received 30,000 all together).[2] On November 27, 1964, the tapes were sent to the manufacturer for the production of the master disc.[3] The album would be released to take advantage of the holiday sales. An advertisement was scheduled for November 17 in *L'Unità*, but was postponed.[4] The album would only arrive in stores in early January 1965, ahead of the spring repeat performances of the show.

It is hard to measure impact of *Bella Ciao* on the Italian record market: we do not have official sales data, although the members of the NCI have always spoken of it as a "successful LP, the first and perhaps only real bestseller" of folk revival and political music (Straniero 1971: 278). In the first months of 1965, there were numerous letters from the NCI to the manufacturing company requesting reissues. On January 26, 1965, for example, a few weeks after publication, an order for 500 additional copies was raised to 1,000 by urgent request, "since the launch of the disc is in full gear, and we are receiving orders we cannot fulfill."[5] Straniero writes at the end of February:

> The record is doing well, selling at a very fast pace, and receiving warm acclaim everywhere. The show . . . will help to push sales even further and make it one of the bestsellers of the year, and our bestseller of all time.[6]

Bella Ciao also appears in the section dedicated to "new releases with high sales potential" in the January 1965 issue of the trade publication *Musica e Dischi*, showing evidence of mainstream attention. The reissues would be constant, even into the 1970s. In 1971, Bosio mentions 30,000 copies sold[7] up to that point. Later, Bermani (1997: 69) estimates sales totaling 100,000 copies, compared to the 10,000 for the other albums of the label.[8]

These numbers are not comparable to pop productions of the same period. The business model of I Dischi del Sole followed almost artisanal methods, suitable for a small independent record company. Once a new record had been created, it proceeded to a first release—usually 1000 copies—and then to continuous reissues of the titles running low. It was a strategy that allowed the company to save on storage and avoid exposing itself economically in the absence of liquidity. This method, however, significantly increased production costs and limited distribution, already hampered by the censorship of state radio and television, which would not broadcast political songs.

The decision to produce discs with high-quality packaging and a rich critical apparatus is understandable from this perspective. I Dischi del Sole record covers were almost always designed by the studio of Giancarlo Iliprandi, one of the most influential art directors of the boom years. *Bella Ciao*, as the first album, set a standard of elegance and graphic simplicity which would characterize much of the subsequent history of the label. The cover is dominated by a photo of the Spoleto show, with the performers reduced to gray silhouettes, isolated from a similarly colored background by a red frame, and above it the inscription "Bella Ciao" in large white upper-case letters (one of the "signatures" of Iliprandi). In the first editions, the cover was glued onto a rigid black canvas board, thicker than normal covers, which provides a second external frame enclosing the whole image. While certainly not economical, it is an original design of extreme simplicity which communicates a feeling of sturdiness and attention to detail. It also demonstrates that, in order to make their business sustainable, I Dischi del Sole must market themselves to a niche audience, willing to buy expensive LPs at a time when the album format is still used primarily for classical music and jazz.

Things were changing, however. New music labeled as "folk" was appearing on the Italian market, mainly imported from the United States. Bob Dylan, Joan Baez, Donovan, Barry McGuire, the Minstrels, and others gained popularity in 1965. From 1966 onward, the national music industry began to support a *folk italiano* that borrowed the Anglophone model of acoustic guitar arrangements and politically engaged texts. Famous stars such as Gianni Morandi and Adriano Celentano published folk-inspired songs that reached the top of the charts (Tomatis 2019: 308–28).

This new mainstream interest in "folk" can be read, much like the activity of the NCI and I Dischi del Sole in the years immediately preceding it, as a project of class distinction, which now included a portion of the youth community, and, at least in part, represented a politicization of the community itself, although—unlike the NCI—the new *folk italiano* movement simply embraced a generic pacifism, without any of the more radical positions. *Bella Ciao*, however, should not be read as a phenomenon separate from the "folk craze." The

NCI was well aware of being a driving force of the changes that were sweeping through Italian popular music. In a 1966 letter, Nanni Ricordi recalls that I Dischi del Sole had in just a few years issued "hundreds of thousands of copies," working toward "achieving a place of respect in the youth market" and "creating the market shift we are now witnessing: folk, protest music, etc." and the "growing sales of 'alternative' records."[9]

This reveals a fundamental paradox that marked the activity of the NCI: in order for its antagonistic discography project to exist, the group was forced to rely on the same market system it was attempting to subvert. The mission of I Dischi del Sole was the political acculturation of the subaltern classes, giving them a voice through recording and revival. To do so, it was necessary to reach the masses by pursuing a project of cultural hegemony. Already by the end of 1964, Bosio affirmed that the time was ripe to "occupy the market quantitatively, substantially, with I Dischi del Sole; to transform a cultural success into an economic phenomenon of such a size as to discourage competition."[10] And yet, adhering to the rules of capitalism meant being overwhelmed by them: there can be no antagonistic content within the market system, because it normalizes and engulfs every voice of dissent. Accepting the "integration of the product we collect and offer" meant "emptying the product itself of any dissenting or expressive significance."[11] Straniero clarified:

> Of course, the system can swallow up even revolutionary songs; actually, you want me to be honest? In my opinion, the system has already swallowed them, swallows them every day. . . . we are not "out of the system" once and for all and forever; no one is going to save our souls.[12]

Adherence or non-adherence to the market system had implications of an ideological, ethical and aesthetic nature. To be "good," folk music must be "real." The "real" folk, according to the NCI, was autonomous and antagonistic. Everything else was "fake folk," controlled by "capitalism" and therefore reactionary. In the midst of folk's explosion into the mainstream, the NCI's cultural struggle shifted its focus to hegemony within the realm of interpretations of folk itself, in order to construct a sense of "authenticity" that is central to the aesthetics of popular music (Moore 2002; Taylor and Barker 2007) and the folk revival in particular. The construction of authenticity always occurs by means of identifying what is "inauthentic" (Bohlman 1988), and the folk revival is defined through the "delegitimization" of competing interpretations of what is "real" folk (Plastino 2016: 37). Delegitimization is both ideological—all the music circulating in the market system is branded as "inauthentic"—and stylistic—it concerns the way in which music is sung and played.

Hence, in the mid-1960s, *Bella Ciao* moved beyond the niche intellectual environment to claim a central place in the newly developing folk canon. Thanks to the album's success and the "Spoleto scandal," it stood as an ideological and stylistic model of "real" Italian folk music: which repertoires should be included; how they should be staged; how they should be performed, sung, recorded in the studio; how they should sound on record; how field research should be done and how revivalists should learn the pieces they perform. These aspects—which can be interpreted as a means of *performing* authenticity, on stage and on record—are the subject of the second part of the book.

PART II

The Performance of "Real" Folk

10 Organizing Folk
The Structure

The structure of *Bella Ciao* is that of a theatrical program of songs, following the model for an "Italian way to *cabaret*" (Eco 1963: 29), which director Filippo Crivelli had cultivated since the early 1960s, particularly at the Teatro Gerolamo, in Milan. Crivelli had had the opportunity to develop this approach in 1960 with the show *Giro a vuoto* featuring singer and actress Laura Betti, and had refined it with the success of *Milanin Milanon*. *Bella Ciao* represented a new development in this line, now applied to the folk revival movement. In fact, the folk revival's modes of representation should also be read as theatrical strategies, which respond to codes developed in the context of cabaret and *canzone milanese* (Milanese song) (Sala 2015). In an article published one year before *Bella Ciao*, Crivelli (1963) offers some guidance on how to build "a show composed of songs." The pace must be "relentless" and "the juxtaposition of the songs must be done in contrasts." "Introductions and explanations" should not be included because they are "useless, sometimes annoying, and above all ineffective."

Following this model, Crivelli and Leydi chose to organize *Bella Ciao* into thematic blocks. A hand-annotated sheet[1] shows their first attempt to divide the songs into categories:

"Work," "Leisure," "War," "Politics," "New songs" (which would then be excluded), "Love," "Prison," etc. In the end, the show was split into two parts: the first contained *Canti di lavoro* (Work songs) and *Canti della domenica* (Sunday songs); the second, more varied, *Canti d'amore* (Love songs), *Canti di carcere* (Prison songs), *Canti contro la guerra* (Anti-war songs), and *Canti politici e sociali* (Political and social songs).

The final setlist was rehearsed for the first time at the Teatro Caio Melisso, as confirmed by the letters and telegrams which Michele Straniero, in his role as internal coordinator at the NCI, sent to the other performers: the group met in Spoleto on June 15, and it is there that "the presentations, the structure of the show, etc."[2] were decided. As Crivelli (1963: 40) explains, in the *cabaret* model the songs can be freely moved, eliminated, or replaced based on audience reactions. The live recordings we have of the Milanese performances[3] confirm that some songs remained fixed—"Gorizia" and "La lega," for example, in the absence of Sandra Mantovani, were performed respectively by Hana Roth and Giovanna Marini—while others were interchangeable.

The 33 rpm follows the structure of the original show, with the two parts each constituting the A side and the B side, but with some obligatory cuts, given the technical limits of the album format. The record contains about 27 minutes of music per side, much more than a standard-length LP in 1965 (the theater shows in Milan lasted around 90 minutes).

Both the album and the show open with a field recording about thirty seconds in length, entitled "La lizza delle Apuane." It is a fragment of a piece sung by workers in Carrara, in the Alpi Apuane area (Tuscany), engaged in the *lizzatura* (that is, the transport of cut marble blocks on sledges). It was recorded by Lomax on December 20, 1954, and was included on the Columbia compilation *Northern and Central Italy* (Lomax and Carpitella 1957a) under the title "Marble Workers' Song." However, the source was never reported, either in the theatrical programs or on the album. Lomax complained of this to Carpitella (Plastino 2016: 34). It is a significant "oversight," given the attention which Leydi and the other members of the group devoted to the scholarly aspect of their work.

"La lizza della Apuane" is a rather typical example of a song meant to provide rhythmic coordination for collective work, as some work songs of the American and African American repertoire do. The latter reference would not have escaped Leydi: one can hypothesize a conscious reference to that world, also in the wake of the *Black Nativity* precedent. Significantly, the other "work songs" do not follow that model. The tracklist opens with a montage between two versions of "Bella Ciao." Giovanna Daffini begins with a slow and sorrowful version of "Bella Ciao delle mondine." A "fade in" starts, and the other performers, clapping along in a more sustained beat, sing the partisan version of the song, on the upbeat swing provided by De Lama's guitar. The following songs, just like "Bella Ciao delle mondine," lament the arduous conditions of the workers: olive pickers ("Cade l'uliva" [The olive falls]), day laborers (Gli scariolanti), *filandere* or textile workers ("Povre filandere" [Poor *filandere*]), and rice-pickers again ("Sciur padron da li beli braghi bianchi" [Mister master with the nice white pants]).

After the work songs is the first of only two[4] spoken sections, recorded on tape by the actor Orazio Orlando. It is an excerpt from a text by the poet Franco Fortini, written expressly for the show. It also appears on the album cover, under the title.

> Sometimes, from the frescoes and paintings, their faces stare out at us. But in books, you almost never hear their voice. Their generations have formed the language we speak, the syntax of our thoughts, the skyline of our cities, the present. But the consciousness which, year after year, harvest after harvest, and stone after stone, they created in their lords and masters, that consciousness did not recognize them. It omitted them. It confused their voices with those of trees or farm animals. At most these songs were heard—when they were heard at all— as the voice of a separate and archaic culture. But today we know that they express the world of the dominated, in protest and in response.

The "Sunday songs" section opens with a montage of *stornelli* (a type of improvised poetry) from the area of Mugello (Tuscany) and Ciociaria (Lazio). Alternating with these are songs of a very different tone, playful ("La mia mama voeul chi fila," in Piedmontese [My mom wants me to spin]), with lyrics that are either salacious ("Pellegrin che vien da Roma" [The pilgrim coming from Rome]) or dramatic ("Il tragico naufragio della nave Sirio" [The tragic shipwreck of the Sirio]), up to the collective conclusion of the first part with "El piscinin" (The little one), a nursery rhyme in Lombard dialect in which each performer has the opportunity to sing a verse, taking turns at the front of the stage.

After the intermission (or after turning over the record), the second part opens with the "Love songs" (again set in the rice paddies, with examples such as "Amore mio non piangere"

[My love don't you cry]), followed by the "Prison songs": "Porta Romana" (the name of a neighborhood in Milan) and "A 'ttocchi a 'ttocchi" (Stroke to stroke) from the Roman repertoire. The second excerpt from Fortini's text introduces the "Anti-war songs."

> Closely intertwined with the history of our country, as with all countries, there is a counter-history. The voices that have echoed one another, from mother to daughter, from boatyard to tilling field, from the barracks to the trenches, from strikes to emigration: they are the testimony of that history.

On the album, the war section is reduced to only two songs as opposed to the four sung in Spoleto: in addition to "Gorizia," there is "Partire partirò partir bisogna" (I will leave, leave I must). We then move on to "Political and social songs," with "Addio a Lugano," sung together by all the performers, "Son cieco," and "La lega." The "Finale" mirrors the beginning, with a repetition of the same sequence in reverse: "Cade l'uliva," (with a different text), the two "Bella Ciao" versions still overlapping, and finally "La lizza delle Apuane."

11 Curating Folk
The Repertoire

As one might guess by browsing through the tracklist, *Bella Ciao* is an anthology compiled in the name of heterogeneity: it is difficult to find any common stylistic or historical denominator between the different pieces. Different eras and contexts coexist, with a preponderance for the late nineteenth and early twentieth centuries. "Partire partirò partir bisogna," as the album notes explain, is a "song of the Napoleonic conscripts of 1799," taken up once again during the nineteenth century. "Addio a Lugano," written by Pietro Gori in 1894, and "Inno della rivolta" (The uprising anthem), linked to the Lunigiana riots of January 1894 (which appeared in the 1965 shows) are anarchist anthems. Several songs come from the repertoire of the *cantastorie*, the itinerant storytellers: for example, "El piscinin," which was a staple of Barbapedana, the Milanese *cantastorie* Enrico Molaschi, active at the end of the nineteenth century. "Il tragico naufragio della nave Sirio" refers to a news story from 1906 (the sinking of a steamer that transported emigrants to America). Some songs can be traced to dances of the area between France and northwestern Italy, such as "La mia mama voeul chi fila," or "Jolicoeur," which seems to be "typical of eighteenth-century French music" (NCI 1964). Some *ballate epico-liriche* (epic-lyrical ballads), which Leydi was investigating in those years, are included in the 1965 shows: "La Pinotta," for example, which is mentioned in the important collection of folk poetry from Piedmont by Costantino Nigra ([1888] 2009), and was recorded on site in Asti, sung by the housewife Teresa Viarengo. Even "Bella Ciao" would have its roots in some ancient ballads, in particular "Fior di tomba" (Tomb flower), "known throughout northern and central Italy," and "La bevanda sonnifera" (The somniferous beverage) (NCI 1965b), both mentioned in Nigra's collection. The sources of the materials, as well, are quite varied and include collections of folk songs compiled by nineteenth-century folklorists, broadsides, and field recordings. Occasionally, the source is Lomax: such is the case with "Canto della Pasquetta" (Easter Monday song) (NCI 1965b) or "Ragazza che risplendi" (Girl that shines), a song from the Albanian communities of Calabria added in the 1965 performances (Lomax and Carpitella 1957a).

The heterogeneity of the repertoire is also due to circumstance. The show was assembled quickly, and it was likely that the performers would be invited to sing songs they already knew. In fact, the songs for the most part had already appeared in previous NCI shows, and many had already been recorded by I Dischi del Sole. The performers' origins also influenced the choice of regional representation: Caterina Bueno was from Tuscany; Daffini and the Piadena from Emilia; Michele Straniero from Piedmont; Sandra Mantovani, Cati Mattea, and Silvia Malagugini from Lombardy; Giovanna Marini and Maria Teresa Bulciolu from central Italy. Bulciolu also handled the few Sardinian songs, limited to "In su Monte Gonare" (On the Mount Gonare) on disc. The north, and in particular the Po Valley, was therefore overrepresented, while areas that had been the subject of earlier research campaigns, such as Puglia, Lucania, Liguria, and Sicily, are completely missing. In short, *Bella Ciao* provides only a very partial picture of the variety of Italy's music, and of the state of the art of field research.

The stylistic and historical differences of the various pieces, of course, did not escape the notice of NCI's theorists. Even beyond *Bella Ciao*, they focused on the need to blend materials collected in the field with the newly composed political songs which the NCI was recording and disseminating. In an article a few months prior to Spoleto, Bosio (1964: 3, 8) admitted that the "the combination of old and new, the mixture of dialect and cultured language, of anonymous and authored texts, might appear to be arbitrary choices." This "appearance of arbitrariness," however, represents "the markings of a reality that is in the process of being composed," and precisely in terms of the problems posed by the *canto sociale*, it is necessary to create "a new definition of the culture of the people's world." The problem of harmonizing the "oldest Po Valley social song" with the new political compositions by NCI's singer-songwriters (1964: 4), but also that of combining the various materials of *Bella Ciao*, is resolved by changing the definition of what folklore is, and what *canto sociale* is; and making the two concepts coincide.

The heterogeneity of the materials is therefore critical to Crivelli's theatrical project and to that juxtaposition of the songs "in contrasts," and at the same time supports and reinforces the political project of the NCI. The Spoleto controversy is partly a consequence of these decisions: if the fuse was "Gorizia," the fact that the song was placed next to other sweeter and *seemingly* non-political pieces was fuel for the fire of scandal. As the reviewers noted, some of those who applauded the love songs, the *stornelli*, the nursery rhymes in the first half, were the ones who later protested against the war songs (Cipriani 1964). In short, the structure of the show seems intended to magnify the unsettling and provocative effect of the second part. In doing so, it reveals the overarching idea behind the project: those who sing in the tavern and croon of love, and those who curse the officers and masters, *are the same voices*. *Bella Ciao* is designed to reinforce the basic thesis of the NCI: namely, the alterity of folk music and its antagonistic nature, regardless of the content of the songs.

Nevertheless, it is not correct to read *Bella Ciao* solely as a show built around a thesis. On the contrary, it plays a central role in the construction of the thesis itself. In Bosio's and Leydi's intellectual journey, their interest in *canto sociale* and protest songs *anticipates* theorizations on folk culture as antagonistic, as well as ideas on the folk revival (Leydi 1960; Bosio and Leydi 1963; Tomatis 2016b: 1061). *Bella Ciao*, thanks to its scandalous success, helps to define the ideology of folk supported by the NCI: the controversies are there to demonstrate that the antagonistic thesis is correct, that folklore is political.

Bella Ciao has therefore constructed its internal coherence through theatrical mechanisms, in close relation with the political and methodological reflections of the NCI; in turn, the NCI defines its theses on the antagonism of folk in relation to *Bella Ciao* and its controversial success. An important piece of this journey is based on the song—or rather, the songs—from which the show takes its title.

Curating Folk

63

12 "Bella Ciao" of the Partisans

In the show and on the recording, there are two different versions of "Bella Ciao," merged together and strategically placed at the opening and the conclusion. The first is the so-called "Bella Ciao delle mondine," a work song belonging to the repertoire of female rice-pickers.

> Alla mattina, appena alzata, o bella ciao, bella ciao, bella ciao, ciao, ciao
> Alla mattina, appena alzata, in risaia mi tocca andar.

> (In the morning, as soon as I rise, o bella ciao, bella ciao, bella ciao, ciao, ciao
> In the morning, as soon as I rise, to the paddy field I must go).

The second is the better-known partisan "Bella Ciao."

> Una mattina mi sono alzato, o bella ciao, bella ciao, bella ciao, ciao, ciao
> Questa mattina mi sono alzato e ho trovato l'invasor.

> (One morning I rose, o bella ciao, bella ciao, bella ciao, ciao, ciao
> This morning I rose and I found the invader).

Given the importance which "Bella Ciao" has acquired over the years—as the anthem par excellence of the Resistance in Italy, and as a song of freedom in much of the world—it is essential to dedicate an excursus to its history. This is important, as well, because some of the peculiarities of the NCI's vision and the *Bella Ciao* project are built around the song's history and its (erroneous) interpretations.

Reconstructing the history of "Bella Ciao" is particularly complex for several reasons. First of all, in contemporary Italy it is considered a divisive song, a symbol of an anti-fascist and leftist identity, and as such it is constantly at the center of controversy. The fact that "Bella Ciao" is—or is not—sung on certain occasions, from political ceremonies to funerals to demonstrations, is in itself a political stance. Second, research on "Bella Ciao" still struggles under the influence of philologically based studies on folk music and is bound within rigid and ideological categories: for example, the exclusive opposition between "folk" and "popular music."

The most complete study on the origins and history of the song is one carried out over a number of years by Cesare Bermani (2020), first in the context of the NCI, and later independently. Most of the numerous books and articles published on "Bella Ciao" use his research as a starting point (Pestelli 2016; Flores 2020). On the other hand, there are hardly any reflections or research on "Bella Ciao" as a *popular* subject, on the modalities of its global diffusion, on its recording history, and on the complex story of its reception.

The great attention paid to "Bella Ciao" in non-academic contexts has contributed to fueling questionable interpretations or those which current research has discredited. For example, the idea that "Bella Ciao" was not sung during the Resistance is still widespread, although its circulation around 1945 is now proven. In fact, the confusion around "Bella Ciao" had already begun in the 1960s. The song was included in the pioneering collection *Canti della Resistenza italiana* (Songs of the Italian Resistance) (1960: 148), in which Leydi participated, where it is stated that "during the Resistance it began to circulate widely within a short time." In the theater program for *Bella Ciao* in Milan, we instead read that "there is no evidence that it was sung during the partisan war" (NCI 1965b), and the same opinion is proposed in the liner notes of the NCI EP *Canti della Resistenza italiana 2*, edited by Leydi (Various 1963). The idea that "Bella Ciao" was not sung in the years of the Liberation most likely occurred because it was not among the most widespread partisan songs. Or rather, it was not one of the most widespread songs among the partisans of northern Italy, whose actions are at the center of the postwar resistance narratives, in literature, and in historiographical reconstructions. On the contrary, it is easy to find traces of other songs, above all "Fischia il vento" (The wind blows), a song composed by the partisan Felice Cascione to the tune of the Russian song "Katiuscia," which was the undisputed anthem of the communist partisans (Bermani 2020: 7–15).

Recent studies have suggested that the first region where "Bella Ciao" began to circulate would have been the central Marches. There is evidence of it being sung in a letter dated April 1946, in which a former Russian fighter, interned in England, writes to a comrade in the Marches, recalling the "young boys who went to die singing the song 'Bella Ciao'"; and in a pamphlet from July 1945, which quotes a "battle song" whose lyrics are similar to the well-known words of "Bella Ciao" (Giacomini 2021: 20, 26). "Bella Ciao" would then move up the peninsula, perhaps due to the partisans of the Maiella Brigade, who would have learned it in the Marches and brought it north on their journey to the front (the Maiella is a region of Abruzzo, south of the Marches). The song would then spread orally from one partisan group to another. Bermani (2020) cites oral sources that place the song in various areas of the north between 1944 and 1945; however, these are testimonies collected in recent years, or in any case after the song's success in the 1960s, and therefore should be evaluated with caution. This is especially true since, after the Liberation, "Bella Ciao" seems to disappear for a few years: it is not included in the earliest collections of partisan songs, and there is no trace of it until 1953.

One of the first references to the song is in the journal of history and folk literature *La Lapa*. In a piece entitled "Folklore della Resistenza" (Resistance's folklore) Cirese (1953) notes for the first time the link between the text of "Bella Ciao" and that of the ballad "Fior di tomba." The following year brings the first publication of the song's musical score in a collection of mountain songs (Bermani 2020: 22).

However, in the years between 1945 and 1953, "Bella Ciao" continued to be sung, and it spread around the world. Testimony published in *L'Unità*, for example, places it in North Korea in 1953, sung by a Korean girl who—according to the newspaper's correspondent—had learned it "from a group of Chinese volunteers" (Longone 1953). Another mentions it among the songs sung during the Indonesian Communist Party Congress in 1959 (Boffa 1959).

The vehicle of international success for "Bella Ciao" is most likely the World Youth Festivals, organized by the World Federation of Democratic Youth beginning in 1947. Despite the lack of clear evidence for the presence of "Bella Ciao" in those contexts—Bermani (2020: 72) reports the information but does not produce supporting sources—it is reasonable to assume that the song would circulate there, given that music was an important component of the interaction between activists from different countries. The envoy from *L'Unità* at the first festival, held in Prague, recounts how "all night, on the banks of the Vltava, folk songs from every country were heard," and that the numerous former Italian partisans "sang, for a long time, together with their Greek brothers" (Ricci 1947). It is therefore highly likely that "Bella Ciao" was part of the repertoire in Prague and in the following years in Budapest (1949) and East Berlin (1951). In light of this success, Enrico Berlinguer's choice to gift a copy of the NCI album to Hồ Chí Minh in 1966 makes sense: the song must have already been known even among Vietnamese communists.

With the 1960s began a new chapter in the story of "Bella Ciao." Its circulation, primarily oral up to this moment, changed hands into recorded format. Not coincidentally, the first known recordings of the song coincided with the boom of the music industry at the beginning of the decade. The twentieth anniversary of the Resistance, in 1965, provided further impetus for the production of shows and records on the subject. Many songs made a generational leap and reached new activists. In the immediate postwar period, the resistance repertoire showed clear local and political variations. Thanks to shows and recordings, a national and shared canon of "songs of the Resistance" could now be codified, one that has remained substantially unchanged even today. At the center now stands "Bella Ciao." It is, in fact, a song well suited to an ecumenical narrative of the Resistance as a meeting place of various democratic and anti-fascist political forces, such as those supported by the new Italian Republic, especially in the 1960s. The text is neutral enough not to assume any particular political hue. It takes up certain *topòi* from the epic-lyrical ballad (the flower on the tomb; the incipit "one morning I woke up"), and its only connection with the reality of war is in the mention of a generic "partisan who died for freedom." On the contrary, "Fischia il vento" was far too closely associated with the PCI to be accepted as a communal anthem, with its references to the "red spring" and the "sun of tomorrow." The events of Spoleto, in any case, contribute to building the political credibility of "Bella Ciao," even in antagonistic contexts: in 1964, at the Algiers Youth Festival, it was sung by Trotskyists and Maoists as a "symbol of anti-fascist youth radicalism" (Flores 2020: 21). The success of "Bella Ciao" is not, however, due only to the ecumenism of its lyrics or to the radicalism they evoked; the catchiness of its melody and the ease with which it can be memorized also guarantee its popularity outside activist circles.

The first known recording of the song was by the popular French singer Yves Montand (1962). Montand, of Italian origin (his true name was Ivo Livi, born in Tuscany), included the piece in a 1962 EP sung entirely in Italian, which was released in France and Italy. Here "Bella Ciao" is combined with other, lighter tunes associated with the repertoire of mountain songs, such as "Amor dammi quel fazzolettino" (Give me that handkerchief, love). The arrangement includes a very "French" accordion and a guitar performing a rhythmic swing clearly of *jazz manouche* derivation, which in the same years is also found, for example, in Georges Brassens and other French singer-songwriters popular in Italy. The bass line is also typical of a jazz-blues sound (it resembles, in the opening bars, the riff of "Hit the Road Jack" by Ray Charles, released a year earlier).

In 1963, "Bella Ciao" was included on the first discs dedicated to the partisan songbook. Released that year was the first recording produced by the NCI, on the second volume of 7-inch vinyl records within the series *Canti della Resistenza italiana* (Various 1963). It is a rather peculiar version, arranged by the former Cantacronache member Fausto Amodei and sung together with Sandra Mantovani, with two harmonized voices and a guitar arrangement very similar to that of Montand. The same swing rhythm is also used, which would later appear in the theatrical version and on the album of *Bella Ciao*, played by Gaspare De Lama. Again in 1963, another of the earliest known recordings appeared (Coro ARCI 1963). In October the song debuted on TV in the broadcast *Canzoniere minimo*, conducted by singer-songwriter Giorgio Gaber (and perhaps it had already been used to introduce "the films of the Resistance on television"; Busetti 1964).

Montand's and the NCI's recordings provided an early model. Yet, in the same years "Bella Ciao" appeared in numerous versions, both in Italy and abroad. In 1965 alone it was recorded by the American group The Minstrels (1965), who in the same year participated in the Sanremo Festival (among the group's singers was Barry McGuire); by Los Marcellos Ferial (1965), with "de-partisanized" lyrics; by the singer Milva (1965), who also included it in her successful show *Canti della libertà* (Songs of freedom); and by Giorgio Gaber (1965). A bizarre Swedish twist-style cover, "Jag är förälskad" sung by Marianne Nilsson (1963?) which uses only the melody (the title means "I'm in love"), dates back to a few years earlier (1962, or more likely 1963).

The success of the NCI must therefore be understood in relation to the new popularity of "Bella Ciao" in those same years. Already in 1964, Michele Straniero reflected on how much of the success of Montand's version was due to the Spoleto scandal.[1] The opposite, of course, is also—or above all—true: "Bella Ciao" emerged in the midst of the folk revival boom in Italy. As *Billboard* explains in listing the new recordings of the song in 1965: "Italian folk ballads seem to be the new vein" (Ruschetto 1965).

13 "Bella Ciao" of the Rice-Pickers

As ironic as it may seem, "Bella Ciao" is a foreign element within the show *Bella Ciao*. It is by far the most recent song, the only one dating after the 1920s. It is the only song dedicated to the Resistance, as well as "not the most significant" of the program, as Daniele Ionio (1965) noted in *L'Unità*. The reason for its inclusion, in a key position and even as the title itself is explained by its kinship with the ancient ballads, but above all by its alleged descent from a work song, the so-called "Bella Ciao delle mondine." One year after the debut, this ancestry would turn out to be false.

In August 1962, Bosio and Leydi had recorded, at Giovanna Daffini's house, a "Bella Ciao" with lyrics that differed from the well-known partisan text, which the singer claimed to have sung around 1932–3—during the fascist rule—when she collected rice in the Vercelli area. The song lamented the difficult working conditions in the rice paddies, "among insects and mosquitoes." On that occasion Daffini recorded the tune with a variation: the omitted repetition of "Bella" in the refrain, which results in an irregular meter. The recording was immediately released on disc, with a critical note that underscored the exceptional nature of the discovery, suggesting this version to be the ancestor of the partisan "Bella

Ciao" (Various 1962). In a subsequent interview with Bermani, in March 1964, Daffini recorded a new version of the same song, this time sung correctly and which she reported having learned in the province of Novara in 1940 (Bermani 1965; 1975; 2020).

Despite Daffini's contradiction and the absence of other sources, the rice-picker origin of "Bella Ciao" was taken for granted. It was perfectly consistent with the folk ideology proposed by the NCI. In the first place, it allowed the NCI to demonstrate "an element of protest . . . active at the peak of fascism" (Leydi in Various 1962), and therefore to reread the relationship between the working classes and the regime. Secondly, it demonstrated a direct filiation between the class consciousness of agricultural workers and partisan warfare, and represented the "missing link" that proved the validity of the entire critical and ideological approach of the NCI, since it created a connection between the "traditional" epic-lyrical ballad and the Resistance, by means of the work song. It was, in short, a classic discovery "too good to be true." And, in fact, it was not true.

At the end of April 1965, on the eve of the Milanese repeat performances of *Bella Ciao*, a letter arrived at *L'Unità*. It was written by a former rice-picker, Vasco Scansani, who lived in Giovanna Daffini's village: he claimed to be the author of "Bella Ciao delle mondine" and provided several pieces of evidence to make his case. He had written it in 1951 or 1952, based on the melody of the well-known partisan song, for a singing competition between teams of rice-pickers in which Daffini had also participated; she likely had learned it on that occasion. Gianni Bosio requested that *L'Unità* not make the letter public, because the news, if disclosed, would have undermined the credibility of the NCI (Bermani 1975; 1992: 31).

In May, a meeting with Scansani was organized in which he clarified the details of the story. Not only was he the true author of the text of the rice-picker version, but Daffini, beginning in 1963, had exploited Scansani's knowledge, learning from him the songs of the rice-pickers which she did not know or no longer remembered. Daffini "paid him with drinks and he sang for her and wrote down the songs," including "Bella Ciao delle mondine" (Bermani 1975: 15). She then proposed those same songs, once learned, to NCI researchers in order to satisfy their requests for "real" pieces of her work song repertoire. Scansani agreed not to disclose the news in exchange for reassurances on the granting of copyrights, although his epistolary exchanges with Bosio show a relationship that was anything but serene.[1] The whole story would be made public only in 1966 and "it was the end of a nightmare" (Bermani 1992: 33).

In retrospect, retracing the NCI interviews with Giovanna Daffini (Bermani 1975), it is easy to recognize the methodological bias that led to misunderstandings. The researchers started from an axiom established *a priori* on the basis of a political motive—namely, the antagonist nature of folk music—and were interested in Daffini providing documents to prove them right. Daffini, for her part, was financially dependent on the concerts and recordings which the NCI guaranteed her, and turned to a repertoire which she did not usually practice.

The thesis that the partisan "Bella Ciao" derived from a work song of the rice-pickers has turned out to be a narrative quite difficult to dispel,[2] and it is not uncommon even today to come across people who believe it to be true, perpetuating the myth in publications and on websites. This occurs, of course, because *Bella Ciao*—whose album cover, never corrected, continues to report the erroneous thesis—is still in circulation, while NCI's late publications remain the subject of scholars. An essay on the affair, which the NCI promised in 1966, was never published (Bermani 1992: 33).

14 Performing Philology
Giovanna Marini's "Fakes"

"Bella Ciao" is not the only case in which NCI researchers were "deceived." Of particular interest are the "fakes" composed by Giovanna Marini. The very concept of folk was built on the idea of "authenticity" in relation to a "tradition" (Gelbart 2007: 153–4), and the Italian folk revival was obsessed with "fidelity" (Plastino 2016: 30). Therefore, one cannot but reflect on the concept of "falseness" in relation to this tradition.

In 1964 Giovanna Marini had recently come into contact with the folk revival movement after having trained in the conservatory, and had not yet developed an awareness of the specificities of oral repertoires, to which she would devote much attention in her later career. As she told ethnomusicologist Ignazio Macchiarella:

> Leydi [. . .] asked me if he could come to my home to hear my songs. He came, and I told him a bunch of lies. I sang things to him, telling him that I had heard them in Abruzzo, that my grandfather was from Abruzzo—he was actually Calabrian—that I had done research in Abruzzo. All things that were complete bull. I don't know why I did it. I didn't have a sense of true and false [. . .] I don't remember the source of the things I sang. (Macchiarella 2005: 35)

The "fakes" included in *Bella Ciao* were "Lu cacciatore Gaetano" (Hunter Gaetano) and "Cade l'uliva." Both were among the most successful songs of the shows: the first was mentioned in numerous reviews as one of the funniest moments, as confirmed by the hearty laughter in the hall which can be heard on the Milanese recordings. The second was strategically placed at the beginning of the album, right after the two "Bella Ciao" renditions, and repeated again at the end. To these examples should be added "Signore cape fammele nu favore" (Mister boss, would you do me a favor), missing from the album but performed in Spoleto and recorded on the EP *I canti del lavoro 4* (Various 1966; Macchiarella 2005: 42).

According to Marini, "Lu cacciatore Gaetano" was created from scratch on the eve of Spoleto (Fabbri, Plastino and Tomatis: 983). It is a playful song that tells of the "miraculous intervention of the Madonna to save a hunter accused of murder," as the liner notes of the album explain. Yet, it appears "completely unrealistic in terms of the peasant tradition," especially for its "swirling articulation of words"; rather, the song seems to *allude* to folklore, offering "an imaginary, sweet and bucolic idea of the music of peasants" (Macchiarella 2005: 43). "Cade l'uliva," for its part, moves "within the most typical tonal scheme" (Macchiarella 2005: 43), following a late nineteenth-century song model (thus, despite being an implausible "fake" of the world it seeks to evoke, its sound aligns with the rest of the program). According to the NCI (1965b), "Cade l'uliva" would be the origin of a later successful "folk-like song," "Lu ciele è chiuse," by the Abruzzese composer Guido Albanese. Logic indicates that the song in question is "Lu piante de le fòjje," composed by Albanese in the early 1920s (Archivio

Albanese 2018), with lyrics by Cesare De Titta, a piece deeply seated in the tonal language typical of the *romanza* (Albanese was in fact the great-grandson of the composer Francesco Paolo Tosti), which later became a standard of the Abruzzese choral repertoire. It is therefore probable that this song was—contrary to what the NCI had suggested—the inspiration for Marini's new composition ("Maybe I had listened to it while skiing"; Macchiarella 2005: 42). However, as with "Bella Ciao," the narrative proposed by the NCI remains dominant in the following years, and Marini's song is now part of Abruzzo's identity.[1]

Macchiarella (2005: 42) notes that the fact that these songs were "'passed off' as 'real' peasant songs from central Italy is indicative of the very vague and superficial knowledge of the music of peasants and shepherds at that time." Rather than arguing about the scientific limitations of the NCI, however, it is interesting to observe how these songs were "authenticated." The theater programs describe their origin and the means of their "discovery" (often in a manner that, in hindsight, seems a little naïve). Of "Lu cacciatore Gaetano" it is said that "Marini learned it in a ski resort in Abruzzo, from the caretaker of a ski lodge who had learned it in Romagna" (NCI 1965b). "Cade l'uliva" is instead a "song of the olive harvesters, still sung today on the plains of Ortona, below the Maiella mountains." The reference to field research in order to authenticate its work characterizes the entire production of the NCI. It is not particularly interesting to question the actual "authenticity" of what the NCI proposed, as this would lead to essentialist interpretations. Rather, it is crucial to understand how such authenticity is *constructed*. On the one hand, *Bella Ciao* is conceived as a political spectacle, and its "truth" concerns its fidelity to the idea of folk as an antagonistic cultural phenomenon. On the other hand, the show also aims to demonstrate the validity of the NCI's scientific research: the tool to demonstrate this "truth" is philology. Even if the songs have been put together in an arbitrary way, often combining different readings, normalizing the variations or even including "fakes," the creative act of the performers and producers must be concealed, hidden behind the objectivity of the "document."

Both the political and philological aspects are constructed through a network of discourses and strategies which concern the paratexts of *Bella Ciao* (the theater programs, the liner notes, the essays of the NCI) as well as the various aspects of staging and recording. We must therefore turn our attention to the different means of *performing* the philological and the political-antagonistic aspects: through staging, arrangements, vocality, methods of acculturation of the performers, and the technical and sound choices related to the recording process.

15 Staging Folk
Direction, Sets, and
Costumes

The absence of video footage—if we exclude some fragments from the Milanese performances (NCI 1965c)—prevents detailed documentation of the performative and visual aspects of *Bella Ciao*. However, we do have the press review of the premiere and the repeat performances, stage photographs (Deichmann 2016), and other materials such as annotated scripts and letters, all of which allow us to reconstruct the general setting.

On the directing front, Crivelli opts for an "extremely simple, essential" staging, with stage action reduced to a minimum and without "facile theatrical effects" (Crivelli 1964). A major point of reference for most Italian musical theater during those years was Bertolt Brecht (1962), whose influence is recognizable in the model of detached performance and "estrangement" of the actors. The video fragments show us the performers in two different modes: an almost hieratic stationary posture in the most dramatic pieces (standing, in a frontal position, arms at their sides, gaze directed forward); and a marked informality during the upbeat songs (sitting in various poses, or standing while clapping their hands and swaying in rhythm).

These are also necessary choices given the short rehearsal time frame, and they respond to the problem of managing non-professional performers (who would probably have had difficulty memorizing and performing overly complex actions). A fundamental role falls, necessarily, on the lighting. Already in Laura Betti's *Giro a vuoto*, Crivelli (1963: 40) had chosen "the simplest solution, but one which nobody (I think) had tried before then: the lights alone would introduce each song." The same operation is perfected in *Bella Ciao*. The tight rhythm of the setlist is punctuated by lighting changes, which invite the audience to focus first on the soloist, leaving the other members sitting in dim light, and then on the entire group in choral pieces.

The scenography, reduced to a minimum, includes a backdrop and sets in gray jute. The choice of a raw and inexpensive fabric is effective in building a neutral space, but it also conveys a certain "impoverished" authenticity from the peasant world. On stage, there are only wooden chairs and benches, important both for the simplicity of the staging and to evoke a tavern space. One of the few stage actions that can be documented refers to that context: during "El piscinin," in the show's Milanese version, Ivan Della Mea and one of the Piadena members play the pub game of *morra*, noisily shouting out the numbers. The seats also act as a mobile set element: they can be gathered "in isolated groups, as a backdrop to an individual at the front, with a choral arch for *stornelli* and humorous songs," and also become "compact to show unity during the most significant songs" (V.B. 1965). Crivelli's stage design is therefore neutral, but it constructs its neutrality by stylizing—in a refined way—some elements of the folk imaginary.

The same applies to stage costumes. Crivelli (1964) decided to present "the performers in their everyday clothes, in a dimension I would call abstract," which avoided both the clichés of the bourgeois *cabaret* and the aestheticization of folklore, that is the typical "folk costumes" that since the nineteenth century had characterized the folk revival. This choice shocked several reviewers: "the performers . . . seem to have wandered on stage by mistake, still wearing their everyday work clothes" (R. B. 1965), while on the Right they spoke of "vesti adeguatamente plebe" (adequately plebeian outfits; G.T. 1964). Nevertheless, those "everyday clothes" are themselves a space of identity construction and class distinction. This is revealed, with powerful evidence, by the recommendations which Straniero sent to the other performers on the eve of his departure for Spoleto. His letter to Bueno, a bourgeois revivalist and cosmopolitan daughter of a Spanish painter and a Swiss writer, specifically asks her not to wear "evening gowns or refined dresses" but instead "simple skirts and blouses, everyday wear."[1] The same is said to Marini, who comes from the Roman bourgeoisie, and to Bulciolu, a university student.[2] Daffini, on the other hand, was asked to bring "that blue dress you wore in Mantua" and "some simple blouse with a skirt: nothing refined, no 'festive attire' [*vestiti della festa*]."[3] The warning against "festive attire" also concerns the Piadena. Straniero writes to Mario Lodi:

> Could you please tell the guys of the Gruppo Padano to bring to Spoleto, as a stage costume, something very simple and clean: pants and dress shirt or t-shirt. Above all, no "festive" clothes or the like, but casual and easy going. All right?[4]

Most likely, the "festive attire" of members of the agricultural proletariat such as the Piadena and Daffini—thus, the "truth" of how Daffini dressed for her concerts, and how the Piadena would have dressed for a special occasion such as a premiere in Spoleto—would have clashed with the need to convey a certain idea of "alterity." Or, more simply, they would have been inelegant, as often are the "festive clothes" of those not used to dressing elegantly (and who do not have money to do so). Once again, "authenticity" must be understood as a construction, obtained through theatrical strategies.

It has been noted how Crivelli's work on *Bella Ciao* marked "a limit, a sense of measure beyond which it was not permissible to go in the representation of alterity"; the choice of a Brechtian detachment in the performance guaranteed "the impetuousness strength of the testimonial as an expression of contemporaneity" and succeeded in the objective of "redeeming the subordinate culture by respecting its distance" (Meandri and Guizzi 2015: 17–18). In fact, there is—as is also recognized by some reviewers (Settimelli 1964b)—an "epic slant" in the staging of some parts of *Bella Ciao*, which abstracts the individual pieces from their historical context, making them, in some way, universal. Again, according to ethnomusicologist Febo Guizzi (Meandri and Guizzi 2015: 18), who echoes Leydi's opinion, it was precisely these directorial choices that contributed to the discomfort of the most reactionary part of the public. On the contrary, Diego Carpitella openly criticized *Bella Ciao* for the way in which it pursued the "conventional, stationary posture of a 'profane' (and socialist) oratory," moreover "entrenching itself within a supposedly philological methodology" (Carpitella [1979] 2016: 460).

16 Strumming Folk
The Arrangements

The attempt to provide a "neutral" and "authentic" dimension to the show is also implemented through sound strategies. In 1958, the Cantacronache had outlined their manifesto. Straniero, along with Sergio Liberovici, clarified how a song had to sound in order to be "real":

> no orchestra, electric instruments, "arrangements." Our songs say real things: in other words, simple. Therefore, even the instrumental accompaniment must be highly natural and simple. All that is needed is a single instrument, chosen from among the most familiar: guitar, accordion, piano. (Straniero and Liberovici 1958)

The search for authenticity—"our songs say real things"—was then linked to a rejection of the arrangement as a *mediation*. This position can be understood in light of the contempt which the left-wing culture of the time harbored toward popular culture and music. The inspiration here is Adorno, who had criticized the practice of arrangement, whose "darkest secret" would be "the compulsion not to leave anything as it is" (Adorno [1938] 2014: 43).

The arrangements in *Bella Ciao* are indeed quite "simple," and once again combine ideological, stylistic, and practical motivations. The only instrumentalist involved is Gaspare De Lama, on acoustic guitar. On stage there are no less than four additional guitars, with steel or nylon strings (this can be deduced from the photos in Deichmann 2016). Giovanna Daffini, Giovanna Marini, Amedeo Merli of the Gruppo Padano di Piadena, Caterina Bueno, and Cati Mattea all play them, mostly accompanying themselves in their respective solo pieces. In the upbeat songs, hand clapping creates the percussion. Other pieces are performed a cappella, with two or more voices.

In Italian popular music up to that point, arrangements for solo guitar were relatively rare. Until the arrival of rock'n'roll in the late 1950s, most songs featured "light music" or big band-like orchestral arrangements, the target of Adorno's criticism. The idea of the performer accompanying him or herself on guitar brought to mind the French *chanson* of figures like Brassens, or anomalous singers like Domenico Modugno, who in the mid-1950s was in fact defined as a *cantante-chitarrista* (singer-guitarist). The expression not only denoted a particular technique—singing accompanied by guitar—but had ideological connotations as well: the *cantante-chitarrista* often wrote and sang refined, socially aware, "authentic" lyrics (Tomatis 2019: 147). The essentiality of the guitar arrangement is, in fact, an invitation to focus on the textual content, and it signals an attempt to elevate the lyrics, even while going against the tradition of Italian popular music up to that time. Meanwhile, the acoustic guitar had also become the iconic sound of American folk music, through figures such as Woody Guthrie and later Bob Dylan.

The research campaigns had already clarified that, in Italy, the guitar was not used extensively in the peasant and

Strumming Folk

85

"traditional" context. It was instead an instrument associated with the figure of the *cantastorie*, typical of the artisan class, and played in taverns (Guizzi 2002: 110). In any case, the prevailing guitar styles in *Bella Ciao* are difficult to justify from a philological perspective. Gaspare De Lama came from a jazz background and tended to accompany the fastest songs with a swing rhythm and strumming technique that stemmed directly from "*la pompe*," a style popularized by Django Reinhardt ("Bella Ciao"— as we have seen—had already received similar treatment by Yves Montand and Fausto Amodei). De Lama's own guitar in Spoleto was a jazz guitar, complete with a pickguard, f-holes, and sunburst finish (in the Milanese performance he would replace it with a "normal" acoustic guitar). During the slow songs, he opted instead for a more delicate accompaniment in a *cantante-chitarrista* style, crucial for "washing away" the nineteenth-century rhetoric from the pieces: "Gorizia," for example, tended toward the sound of Modugno, or Neapolitan singer Roberto Murolo. Marini, in her songs, demonstrated a more "classical" taste, in accordance with her conservatory training. Daffini, for her part, strummed a steel-string guitar, apparently of rather low quality, which in live recordings—in line with her "authentic" character—boasted a rather twangy timber and tuning that was not always impeccable.

The guitar in *Bella Ciao* is therefore necessary to provide a "neutral" accompaniment that places the voices and texts at the fore. At the same time, it evokes both a "folk" authenticity and a refined and fashionable sound, one tied to the French *chanson*, to jazz players and singer-guitarists, in opposition to the kitsch of light orchestral arrangements and the electric sounds of rock'n'roll.

17 Singing and Learning to Sing Folk
The Voices

The alterity and authenticity of folklore which *Bella Ciao* attempts to stage involve particular vocal choices. The specificity of the Italian political folk revival is embodied above all in the politics of the voice: not only what is sung but *how* it is sung.

The NCI was well aware that the voices "of the people," revealed through field research and recorded on tape, represented a point of rupture. They sounded profoundly different from the voices of officials and those heard on the radio: they expressed themselves in different languages, utilized different modes of emission, and at times seemed to operate within entirely different musical systems. The designers of *Bella Ciao* fully understood the potential of those "sharp, harsh, screaming voices," as Morandi ([1965] 2012: 22) commented during the first days in Spoleto: "Spaccavano tutto. Bene" (They broke everything. Good). Marini (2012: 10) has repeatedly described her encounter with Daffini as an epiphany regarding the alterity of the "traditional" modes of expression.

NCI's account of the Spoleto scandal devoted great attention to the shock value—in addition to, or beyond, the content of the songs—of the performers' voices, and that of Daffini in particular. Marini has often recalled a review in which Daffini's voice was described as a "voce da cortile" (a courtyard voice), the "unbearable voice of a strangled throat, like a woman shouting out of a window in the courtyard" (Macchiarella 2005: 48; Marini 2005: 172).[1] Once again, this narrative must be problematized. Daffini was certainly opposed by a part of the public (the "countesses": we may recall the phrase, however apocryphal: "I did not pay two thousand *lire* to come here to the theater and hear my servant sing on stage"). However, it is equally true that critics are almost unanimous in praising her merits. Negative reviews (still in the minority) either stem from right-wing newspapers, and therefore indiscriminately attack the NCI project; or they criticize the raw, amateur performances. The targets of criticism in these cases, however, are the "nice and sophisticated young ladies"—that is, the revivalist singers of the NCI—who are accused of "amateurism" and of singing out of tune (Griffo 1964). The "real" folk performers—Daffini and the Piadena—are almost always praised and recognized as "authentic." Even the conservative *Il Corriere della Sera*, when discussing Daffini, speaks of a voice that has, in itself, "the color of the earth, the mark of the peasant world" (*Il Corriere della Sera* 1965); elsewhere her voice is described as "portentous in the use of falsetto" and endowed with "an acute and instinctive sense of phrasing" (Ciarpaglini 1964). An analysis of the reception of *Bella Ciao* in the press, therefore, suggests that the NCI makes more of the rupture caused by this "authentic" way of singing than its actual impact merits. Once more,

Bella Ciao confirms a self-fulfilling prophecy: its subsequent mythologization as a founding act of the folk revival has also established it as a model of "true" vocality, and has helped to politicize certain modes of singing.

The "political" vocality which the NCI proposed should instead be contextualized and historicized in the broader context of the changes in taste occurring in the early 1960s, which radically affected the models of stardom and the aesthetics of sound, including that of the voice. It is useful to sketch a phylogeny of "authentic" vocality in Italy to understand the cultural context in which the original model of the NCI evolves.

The first politicized theorization of the voice occurred in Italy, once again, with the Cantacronache. According to Straniero and Liberovici (1958), in popular music there was a performative practice operating in which "anything goes": "falsetto, or in any case constant modification of the natural voice," "melodramatic attitudes," or "the imitative provincialism of poorly assimilated international forms." In opposition to these models, Cantacronache presented the "ideal performer." Among the examples to follow are Georges Brassens and Germaine Montero (thus modeled after French singer-songwriters and cabaret performers), Brechtian interpreter Ernst Busch, and the *cantastorie* Ciccio Busacca. The common denominator is an instinctive, untrained—and indeed "authentic"—approach to singing, also in the wake of the neorealist paradigm. The Cantacronache's ideal performer "is not a singer in the typical sense" because "that sort of voice brings to mind a performance overly entrenched in classical training." Rather, it must be "a *folk singer* [*un cantore popolare*].

In other words: a voice that is raw and uncultivated, *but natural, alive, familiar, human*" (Straniero and Liberovici 1958).

Brecht's idea of the "estrangement" of the performer (1962: 23–4) represents a decisive influence. It is also an effective way of interpreting the older songs of the nineteenth century or the First World War which populate *Bella Ciao*: the use of an obsolete and rhetorical Italian, typical of those songs, must be purified of melodramatic tones, and re-semanticized in an epic dimension. Singing that is "detached" and untrained is critical to the goal, just as the minimal guitar arrangements are. At the same time, recognizable in the left-wing culture of these years is a distrust of the "beautiful voice" as part of a more general contempt for popular music. In 1965, while *Bella Ciao* was making the rounds of repeat performances, *Canti della libertà* was staged at the Teatro Lirico in Milan, with singer Milva performing a selection of political songs ("Bella Ciao" included). The show was the polemical target of numerous letters and editorials by members of the NCI. In the pages of the periodical *Vie Nuove*, while singing Milva's praises, the journalist raises a doubt:

> It is difficult to resist her, but it is also difficult not to wonder if this extraordinary instrument [her voice] would not obtain similar results singing, let's say, the praises of tyranny. The participation which Milva solicits is of an exquisitely irrational nature. (Capriolo 1965)

The leftist intellectual, therefore, seems to distrust what is pleasing because it is one of the seductive strategies of mass culture. The "real" antagonistic voice must be harsh, violent, one "that breaks everything."

At any rate, the vocal models of international popular music were also shifting. Ever since the late 1950s in Italy, a new way of singing was gaining popularity, especially thanks to the singer-songwriters and the so-called *urlatori* (howlers). The press attributed this last term, both ironic and derogatory, to young Italian rock'n'roll performers, revealing how the new vocal styles borrowed from African American examples represent a break with traditional Italian song. For young singers, singing in an instinctive manner, perhaps with pronunciation defects or even out of tune, becomes a brand of authenticity which helps to build a new foundation for aesthetic values: the new youth music is "good" because it is "real," it says real things in a real way (Tomatis 2019: 160, 206).

It is precisely in this context that an awareness began to form—thanks to field research—of the presence of "other" vocal qualities in the music of the oral tradition. These voices, which were being recorded and disseminated on disc, could offer a new inspirational stylistic model. The Brechtian "cabaret" style was now being disavowed by the NCI, at least officially. The performers of the folk revival and of *canto sociale* must instead look to the example of "true" folk performers, learning their style through systematic study.

Between 1964 and 1965, after the "Spoleto scandal," Roberto Leydi introduced the categories of *ricalco* (literally, traced impression, rubbing) and *specifico stilistico* (stylistic specific) into the debate. During the Milanese performances of *Bella Ciao*, a cyclostyle pamphlet distributed to the public (Bosio and Leydi [1965] 2016: 114) defined these concepts and positioned them as the scholarly foundation for the show and the NCI's work. Leydi's objective was to identify, through field research and analysis, "a stylistic specific that preserves the traditional document from degradation and adulteration," since "the stylistic fidelity of a new performance of folk songs is a guarantee of contemporaneity and a defense against archaism." The ultimate goal is to "isolate" the "stylistic specific" of a repertoire or a region, but—as Leydi explains—we are still far from the goal. What remains is "the grueling work of *ricalco*, down to the granular level." The revivalist must study the recording and the encounter with the "informant" in order to isolate the formal elements (the melody, the rhythm, the harmony, etc.) but also the vocal techniques, the posture of the body, the expression of the face, the muscular tension, etc. The new performer must not be the "double" of the original performer, but his "contemporary translator" (Bosio and Leydi [1965] 2016: 115).

This model shows several connections with that of Lomax (1959b), who had argued the importance of the "singing style" in the urban revival (his essay is also included in Leydi 1972), and who was already laying the foundations of what would become the project of *Cantometrics* (Lomax 1959a). At the same time, the NCI was in contact with Ewan MacColl, Peggy Seeger, and the London Critics Group, who would also be in Italy in 1966 (Tomatis 2016b). It is easy to recognize some commonalities with what English and American colleagues were producing in those years (and some writings by MacColl and Peggy Seeger are also included in Leydi 1972). In particular, MacColl's acting background introduces into the revival Stanislavsky's "method" for acting and Laban's theories for dance, "adapted for the voice" (Laing 2014: 162), thus seeking a close identification between the revivalist and the subject matter of the revival.

In pursuing the "stylistic specific," the revivalist, from the performative point of view, enacts an interesting but not necessarily conscious semiotic operation. The revivalist, like a classical musician, looks to repertoires and models outside his or her own, those coming from "elsewhere" (Meandri and Guizzi 2015: 17), be it chronologically, geographically, or socio-culturally other. By engaging critically with these models, the revivalist is in fact playing a role with his or her voice, but like any performer is also representing him or herself through that role (Auslander 2006). *Bella Ciao* therefore poses several problems, especially in terms of the coexistence of "authentic" voices and revivalists.

The case of Giovanna Daffini is particularly interesting. Both the NCI and the press present Daffini as a true representative of the folk world (Chiozzi 1965). From a stylistic point of view, Daffini's way of singing was recognized as typical of the rice-pickers of the Po Valley (Mantovani 1966). In fact, NCI scholars realized almost immediately that Daffini's vocality can neither be limited to that world nor taken as a model of folk "purity." A rice-picker in her youth, Daffini came from a family of musicians. Her father, a violinist, occasionally played pop and classical repertoires with an orchestra; he had been a street musician and provided photoplay music for silent films in small village cinemas. Daffini had often accompanied him on guitar, which is what she was doing just before *Bella Ciao* with her husband, Vittorio Carpi, also a violinist. Throughout her life (at the time of *Bella Ciao* she was over fifty years old), Daffini was a semi-professional musician engaged in the local circuit of festivals and weddings, and she tried her hand at a repertoire ranging from hit songs—"Marina" by Rocco Granata, one of the rare recorded examples (Daffini 1975)—to dance music, from opera extracts (Lehár's *The Merry Widow*) to Schubert's *Ave Maria*. The songs of the rice-pickers, in many cases, had not been part of her repertoire for more than thirty years, and had been recovered only due to NCI's initiative (with limits clearly demonstrated by the case of "Bella Ciao"). Thus, she is nothing like the rather naïve character which the newspapers and the NCI created for her (Love 2018: 237). Daffini's peculiar vocal style stands precisely at the intersection of very different musical practices. The elements that jump out most clearly are the "*spinto* voice type" (Marini 1992: 83), the use of melismas, and a very strong vibrato. Daffini seems to have "an almost subproletariat aspiration towards the myth of the opera singer" (Marini 1992: 83) and toward the imitation of radio voices from the war years, above all that of the singer Tonina Torrielli, her declared idol (Leydi 1992: 61). This peculiar style was also formed by the need to "project" her voice to be heard in noisy contexts and without amplification, and had reasonably changed over the years as she aged. However, it is quite evident that Daffini's "stylistic specific," rather than being typical of a single area or repertoire, is on the contrary profoundly idiosyncratic, and is constructed on the complex intersection of primary and secondary orality (Ong 1982), of live and recorded music, of classical, traditional, and popular models.

The main proponent of the *ricalco*, even in the years following *Bella Ciao*, is Sandra Mantovani. Mantovani is given ample space in the performance of *Bella Ciao*, and is repeatedly cited as the main performer of the show. In the theater program, where her name appears first, she is described (probably by Leydi himself) as "one of the most authentic voices" of the Italian revival, "as her style and repertoire are based on direct research experience" (NCI 1964). Mantovani constructed her style, according to her own words (1966; [1972] 2016), from the model of traditional performers recorded in the field. (At the same time, when listening to her perform, one easily recognizes the Brechtian model as well: for example, in "Gorizia"). Leydi and Mantovani attach significant importance to the recording in the process of retracing the stylistic specific, in line with Bosio ([1967] 1998). In an article for a widely circulated weekly, Leydi ([1964] 2016: 552) quotes "a folk singer" (almost certainly Mantovani herself):

> I perform and have recorded many folk songs, but only those which I learned directly from the tapes, from the original recordings—that is, from the voice of the people—are . . . stylistically authentic . . . It is not easy to explain, but I can immediately recognize, when listening to other folk singers, if they have learned their song from written music or from a tape.

The role which recording plays in the acculturation of the *Bella Ciao* performers (and of the folk revival in general) is further complicated by the case of the Gruppo Padano di Piadena. As a NCI press release explains, the group is composed "of three workers who sing songs they have learned from their fathers and their fellow workers."[2] However, from correspondences and various NCI sources, we learn that the Piadena had in many cases learned the songs in their repertoire from recordings which the researchers gave them, indeed obtaining their "best results" precisely "in the pieces taken directly from the recordings, and studied on the tapes" (NCI 1966: 11). At the heart of the "stylistic specific," therefore, is a problematic essentialization of "folk singing." It connects the alterity of folk music, and therefore its own antagonistic value, with a *stylistic* element—that is, a supposedly "correct" way of singing—that should be reconstructed philologically through research and imitation. The paradox lies in the fact that, from this perspective, it is Mantovani who is the most "authentic" performer: more authentic even than the Gruppo Padano di Piadena and Daffini.

While it is intellectually dishonest to dismiss Leydi's model as mere essentialization, in the practice of revival the emphasis on recreating an "authentic" way of singing through the *ricalco* has often become precisely this. For example, Malagugini and Mattea (2016: 523–4) recall that many of the performers of *Bella Ciao*

> had vocal problems, because our attempt to produce the folk vocal emission [*emissione popolare*] was very tiring and the result was often problematic (our singing was all "in the throat"). And so we made steam inhalations with boiling water and baking soda with a towel over our heads, we and Sandra [Mantovani] and Maria Teresa [Bulciolu]. Or strychnine injections, which seem like they should be illegal, but in truth they help treating hoarseness.

Ewan MacColl, in an interview with Vacca (Moore and Vacca 2014: 118–19), recalled as well the use of strychnine, attributing no therapeutic value to it, but instead a true modification of the voice.

> The young Italian singers, the girls . . . were swallowing strychnine to make the vocal cords harsh so the voices would come out and make them sound like peasant singers.

This way of "performing philology" with the aid of chemistry, which, ironically, ends up trivializing and homogenizing the countless differences—stylistic, linguistic, gender, genre—which *Bella Ciao* narrated, is thus affirmed within the new vocal aesthetics of the boom years as the "right" way of singing folk; at the same time, it signals a new aesthetics of "real" vocality which, through the mediation of the recording, moves from *Bella Ciao* to act as a model readily available to all, even beyond the edges of folk music revival.

18 Sounding Folk
The Studio Recording

The trust in the field recording which inspires the acculturation of the revivalists also reverberates in studio practices and in the productions of I Dischi del Sole. The socialist utopia which Bosio ([1967] 1998) pursued had focused on the tape recorder as a democratic tool, enabling oral culture to gain awareness and upend its relationship with the dominant culture. This pro-technological ideology (the tape recorder as an instrument of redemption for the lower classes) coexisted problematically with the general criticism of mass culture and technology which intellectuals had advanced, and with the consequent distrust of the mass media for corrupting the alleged "authenticity" of the message. This prejudice is already found, mixed with the Brechtian model, in the theorizations of the Cantacronache, who were very critical of the microphone.

> The folk singer [*cantore popolare*] is completely separate from the deforming quality of the microphone: it will be up to the audio technician to capture that voice with better results (expressive naturalness). Too many singers today use the recording microphone as if it were a loudspeaker, establishing a direct and necessary relationship with it: this relationship must instead be *indirect and casual*. (Straniero and Liberovici 1958)

In the folk revival, the recording aspires to transparency, as they are considered "as evidence of reality." However, recordings are always "humanly constructed texts" (Ord 2017: 48). The technical choices in the studio or in the field—how to arrange the microphones, how and whether to edit the sound, etc.—are structured by ideologies, and translate into aesthetics of sound.

I Dischi del Sole recordings are more often presented as *documents*. The logic behind the studio sessions of *Bella Ciao* is not to produce an original studio album but, as the liner notes explain (NCI 1965a), to document the Spoleto show in the most faithful way possible. The choice to replicate the setlist, including the repetition of the initial songs at the end, is revealing: it would certainly have made sense to include different songs, or to reduce the duration (in a disc that pushes the technical space limits of the 33 rpm format, the reduction would also have benefited the sound quality).

Like most of I Dischi del Sole albums, *Bella Ciao* is not notable for its sound quality and clearly shows the haste with which it was produced. Several performances include inaccuracies; there are occasional distortions or audio clipping, or perceptible cuts of the tape. In some places—for example, in the "Sunday songs" section—there is an evident attempt to create the sound environment of the tavern, in which the songs are ideally set: disturbances appear in the background, including comments, laughter and gag verses. In general, the record maintains a certain *lo-fi* patina which the cd reissue (NCI 1992) has not diminished much.

The whole album is apparently recorded live in studio, in mono, and without overdubbing. It can be assumed that two or three microphones are used at the same time: one for the main voice (or voices), one for the guitar and (possibly) one for the occasional backup singers. An attentive listen reveals inconsistent microphone and mixing choices, which suggest a production that is not particularly mindful. The guitar is sometimes in the foreground, sometimes it disappears into the background. The reverb is at times applied liberally—in choral pieces, for example, by the Piadena, and in some monodic pieces ("Jolicoeur") or in duets ("In su monte Gonare")—and at other times is almost absent (for example, in the pieces by Daffini). Already very common in Italy at that time, reverb— along with echo—was associated with pop productions and not with the objectivity of folk "documents," as a cosmetic effect that alters the voice and masks the inaccuracies of the performances (Zak 2012). Its use in *Bella Ciao* is therefore particularly significant.

While acknowledging the lack of consistent choices and the production limits, the circumstances (limited budgets and little time available) or the paltry experience of the technicians do not explain everything. The NCI's search for authenticity and its distrust of arrangement seem to be transformed, in the studio, into a programmatic technological "pauperism" (Fabbri 2008: 133). In 1964, the idea of the album as a "studio art recording" (Turino 2008) that does not replicate a live performance but creates something original and "artificial" was just coming to the fore in pop music (Zak 2012). NCI's production choices can be read as deliberately oppositional to those of mainstream pop, similar to what Ord (2017: 154) demonstrated with the sound of Topic records in the UK. However, the NCI had knowledge of recording studio resources and often exploited them with regard to the editing of tapes. Leydi and Bosio were

100

aware of the experimentations in the *Radio Ballads* by Charles Parker, Ewan MacColl, and Peggy Seeger, who since 1958 had employed modernist editing techniques, derived from Soviet cinema, to construct complex narratives of the life of the British working classes, mixing sound, speech, and music. For Leydi in particular, that model must also have revealed an affinity with the Italian avant-garde, of which he had been among the pioneers: in 1955 he had collaborated with the composers Bruno Maderna and Luciano Berio for *Ritratto di città* (Portrait of a city), the first composition of electronic and concrete music made in the RAI Phonology Studio in Milan (Ferraro 2015: 72). He therefore was fully aware of the semantic and creative implications of recorded sound, of noises and field recordings in particular. As the previous quote from Cantacronache also demonstrates, intellectuals interested in music certainly did not overlook the constructed nature of the recordings and their ability to convey meaning.

In particular, the presence of "La lizza delle Apuane" on the disc elicits a reflection: one cannot underestimate the acousmatic power of that fragment, "stolen" from Lomax, for its ability to construct meaning in *Bella Ciao*. As an introductory piece, it acts as a sanction of "truth": it seems to exist in order to remind us that what we are about to hear are the *true* voices of the people, and that the recording is a document of those same voices. And yet, because it is profoundly alien to the rest of the record, both in the timber of the voices and in the "grain" of the recording, it also reveals the recorded, artificial nature of the rest of the album. It seems to declare: "what you are about to listen to is a recording." Moreover—this element was never mentioned by the NCI, nor was it noted by commentators—what we hear is a reworking of the document which Lomax recorded: some repetitions are cut, increasing the rhythm of the incitements by the marble quarrymen and reducing their duration. This would be a *falsification* from the NCI's point of view. Trust in recording as an objective datum coexists, in short, with the awareness of its manipulability, a text produced by humans and not a found object. The ambition to create "authentic," unmediated music coexists with an almost metalinguistic use of recorded sound.

In conclusion, the entire *Bella Ciao* project stages—*performs*—a certain idea of authenticity which is both political (that is, relative to the antagonistic autonomy of folk) and philological (that is, linked to the "truth" of the documents). It does so through directorial, curatorial, musical, vocal, and sound strategies. What results, however, is not a faithful documentation of anything but these very same processes. The *Bella Ciao* album establishes them for posterity, standing as a stylistic and ideological model for those (many) who wish to use it. Its sound—lo-fi, dirty, raw—is a *political* sound: the real sound of folk.

Coda
Us and Them

Our car is shaking, wobbling and stalling on rather difficult roads: but who notices the discomfort, even if the tires pop? An immense canvas in warm and violent colors lies before us: a landscape that is all a smile and a song. The plain meets us with its blue, green and golden tones; the streams unleash their waters with a cheerful boogie-woogie rhythm; the countless farmhouses seem to invite us in, with their doors wide open, from which every day hundreds of beautiful, flourishing girls walk out into the sun . . . The rice-pickers like to sing, to lessen their fatigue or sweeten their repose . . . Songs, songs, songs: everywhere. In the crystal-clear air, in the golden sun, in the coolness of the evening. They repeat the refrains from the Sanremo Festival, and it's so pleasant to have them caress the ear, while the car bumps along, trying to get back onto the highway. (Gianelli 1954)

In 1954, ten years before *Bella Ciao*, the year in which Lomax was touring Italy with his tape recorder, *Sorrisi e Canzoni* (Smiles and songs)—one of the best-selling popular Italian weeklies—launched a "contest" dedicated to the rice-pickers. More of a survey, in truth. The *mondine* had to fill out a slip indicating the song they sang most often in the paddy fields. The prizes included a trip to Rome, a bedroom set, sewing machines, accordions, radios, irons. The cover of the issue featured the beautiful Silvana Mangano, who five years earlier had played a rice-picker (and danced a sensual boogie-woogie) in the film *Riso amaro* (*Bitter Rice*) by Giuseppe De Santis, nominated for the 1950 Oscar for Best Writing. In this same period, Vasco Scansani composed the text of "Bella Ciao delle mondine," and perhaps some of the "flourishing girls" encountered by the correspondents of *Sorrisi e Canzoni* had worked side by side with Giovanna Daffini just a few seasons before. Almost certainly they had gone to see *Riso amaro*.

The fact that the rice-pickers went to the cinema, read *Sorrisi e Canzoni*, sang songs from Sanremo, and danced the boogie-woogie is of course no great discovery. If de Martino (1949: 421) had heralded the "irruption of the subaltern world of the people into history," the irruption was reciprocal: history had also made its grand entrance into the "subaltern world." Far from living in their own bubble, uncontaminated by modernity, the rice-pickers were women of their time. They sang—when they sang: the folk revival has often given the impression that rice-pickers did little else—the songs they enjoyed singing: old songs and new, pop or political, which they learned from their older coworkers or from the radio and from records. Intoned in various styles, handed down orally, or adapted by imitating the singers of Sanremo. Singers like Tonina Torrielli, the idol of Giovanna Daffini, who had been a worker in a candy factory in Novi Ligure, 60 miles south of the rice fields.

Although there were many rice-picker songs recorded by researchers, the fact that the rice-pickers also (or mostly?) sang songs from Sanremo is something we must imagine between the pauses in the tape. The folk revival is an act of selection and curation. First, it discards what is not "authentic," what is contaminated by the "market" and "capitalism." Second—through shows, records, books—it promotes a canon and prescribes a style. What "the people" left behind in the wake of modernization, the revival claimed, collected, cleaned up, arranged, and put back into circulation for its audience, imbuing it with a political and antagonistic aura.

Bella Ciao played a fundamental role in this process. A few years after the album's release, during the 1968 protests, the students occupying the universities sang the songs and composed new lyrics to the music of Giovanna Marini (Gobbi 1988: 62, 67, 82). The old anarchist anthems from the unification period, learned from I Dischi del Sole records, provided the music for new protest songs and for the anthems of the extra-parliamentary Left (Tomatis 2019: 432). The NCI's production became one of the "official" soundtracks of the revolt, through the end of the 1970s when, along with other utopian ideals of that period, I Dischi del Sole failed (Bermani 1997: 157). The political sound of folk influenced activist record productions for quite a long time: performers sang, played the guitar, made recordings in a certain way, because that was the "correct" way to do it. For those who made music and politics, the NCI's huge catalog of critical discourses and sounds represented an "organic body of thought and practice on the political song with which it was necessary to reckon" (Franco Fabbri in Casiraghi 2005: 53). At the center of it all, without any real competitors, stood *Bella Ciao*.

Nevertheless, even the activists who promoted the revival were men and women of their time. If there was a

Coda

common language between the young antagonists of the 1968 Movement, it was not so much folk, but English and American rock (Ortoleva 1998: 73). Those same students, after singing the songs of the rice-pickers, put on an album by the Beatles or Lucio Battisti, perpetuating a "dichotomy" between "the songs that we enjoy for ideological purposes" and those we listen to "in private," as Diego Carpitella (1965) noted, somewhat caustically, in the aftermath of *Bella Ciao*. Meanwhile, though the songs of the rice-pickers were "played in parlors" (Settimelli 1964a) and sung in the occupied universities, the rice-pickers themselves, lacking ideological motivations, continued to listen to pop music and sing the Sanremo tunes.

However, to describe the folk revival solely as a practice limited to the left-wing intellectual bourgeoisie does not account for the complexity of the issue. The other side of this act of selection and curation is, in fact, the encounter with "the other," with "the people." The story of *Bella Ciao* and the NCI recounts the contradictions of a vision and the limits of its implementation, but also the value of a utopian political project that continues to wield great power. As Philip Bohlman (1998: 92) wrote,

the historical dramatis personae of the folk revival was not the folk at all, but rather a privileged swath of . . . society that turned ethnic, class, and social categories inside out in search of themselves—or, more to the point, in search of their own selfness, a reason for that selfness to cohere in goodness.

Again, however, the complementary perspective is overlooked. What did "the folk" think? What did Giovanna Daffini ponder when she saw her photo in the newspapers? After all, the magazines that covered the "Spoleto scandal"—among which *Sorrisi e canzoni* (Neri 1964)—also counted her rice-picker companions among their readers. Some of the most beautiful pages of Morandi's diary are those in which he and the Piadena tell of their very personal encounter with "the other," with intellectuals and with show business: "I try hard to speak in Italian. I can only start the conversation, then I continue in dialect. I always have to translate myself," writes the author in a moment of frustration, and shortly after he notes: "The TV spotlights hurt my eyes" (Morandi [1965] 2012: 23, 24). The Piadena's Delio Chittò states:

> we did not expect much. . . . We learned the songs in the library and thought we would sing at the *feste dell'Unità*, or in the *Avanti!* Festivals, in cooperatives and clubs, make enough for drinks and that's it. But instead! Are we going to do a hundred performances in Vienna? And in London? (Morandi [1965] 2012: 56)

The epistolary exchanges between the Gruppo Padano di Piadena, Giovanna Daffini, and the NCI tell a different story about the production of *Bella Ciao*: a story of social ascent, of real mediations with "the boss" (who threatens to fire his musicians-workers if they miss a shift to do a concert with the NCI[1]), and of pay negotiations for the said concert, but also, a story of people appropriating their own culture, with pride. Years later, Chittò, along with Amedeo Merli, would leave their job as a laborers and found the Duo di Piadena, touring all over the world, recording albums, and performing on television (Bratus et al. 2018), and in the process bringing many of those songs they had learned from the NCI tapes to a truly popular audience. But perhaps, in doing so, they no longer made "real" folk music?

Revivalists who learn songs from the people. The people who learn songs from the recordings of the revivalists. The rice-pickers who sing Sanremo hits and the university students who sing the rice-pickers. Hô Chí Minh listening to *Bella Ciao* 6,000 miles from Spoleto (about that: did he *actually* listen to it?) and my mother singing me NCI's songs as lullabies in the late 1980s. The history of the Italian folk revival, as told through *Bella Ciao*, reveals a complex mirror game on the nature of "the people" and its music—"folk" or "popular," and never have these categories appeared so fuzzy. Who is doing the discovering, and who is being "discovered"? Who is authenticated by whom? After all, who are "we" and who are "they"? Who are "the people" and who are "the masses"? Perhaps the lesson to be drawn here is, once again, the one which Umberto Eco ([1964] 2008: 277) suggested in 1964, the year of *Bella Ciao*, and which Gramsci himself had suggested previously: in many different moments throughout the day, each of us is one of the masses, without exception.

Notes

Chapter 3

1 All quotations in Italian are translated by the author.

Chapter 5

1 NCI 40; LEYDI MI.

2 No trace of this footage remains.

3 Flyer for the Festival dei Due Mondi, Spring 1964, LEYDI MI 71/02/01.

4 Letter, Michele Straniero to Caterina Bueno, June 9, 1964, AVANTI Corrvaria 25.

5 AVANTI Corrvaria 25.

6 Letter, Michele Straniero to Gilberto Bacci, December 31, 1964, GALLO Corrvaria 27. The text appears in Leydi 1960: 15, as well as in some magazines.

Chapter 7

1 For example, Enrico Vaile's comedy *I piedi al caldo* (Provantini 1964).

Chapter 8

1 AVANTI; GALLO; NCI.

2 Letter, NCI (Tullio Savi) to the *Festa dell'Unità* Committee, 31 July 1964, AVANTI Corrvaria 26.

Chapter 9

1 I Dischi del Sole, *Catalogue*, April 1973, IeDM.

2 Letters, Gianni Bosio to the performers of *Bella Ciao*, December 3, 1964, GALLO Corrvaria 27.

3 Letter, Michele Straniero to Leonsolco, November 27, 1964, GALLO Corrvaria 27.

4 Letter, Alberto Gibilterra (*L'Unità*) to Michele Straniero, December 10, 1964, GALLO Corrvaria 27.

5 Letter, Michele Straniero to Leonsolco, January 26, 1965, GALLO Corrvaria 28.

6 Letter, Michele Straniero to Riccardo Landau (*L'Espresso*), February 24, 1965, GALLO Corrvaria 28.

7 Letter, Gianni Bosio to Pietro La Falce (Ri-Fi), February 5, 1971, GALLO Corrvaria 40 (Love 2018: 267).

8 *Bella Ciao* would also be released in France (NCI 1975).

9 Letter, Nanni Ricordi to Giuseppe Pedercini, November 17, 1966, GALLO Corrvaria 35.

10 Gianni Bosio, *Edizioni Avanti!—Nota al bilancio '63–'64*, December 23, 1964, BOSIO B71.

11 Letter, NCI (unsigned) to Mario Alicata, April 30, 1965, NCI 04/05.

12   Letter, Michele Straniero to Andrea Vasile, March 3, 1967, GALLO Corrvaria 36 (Love 2018: 292).

Chapter 10

1   LEYDI MI 02/71/06.

2   Letter, Michele Straniero to Caterina Bueno, June 9, 1964, AVANTI Corrvaria 25.

3   Recordings are available of the performances from May 19 to 22, 1965, in Milan (LEYDI CH 18BD556, 26BD483, 18BD560, 18BD613, 26BD274, 26BD286, 26BD399, 26BD402).

4   Morandi ([1965] 2012: 17) lists three; in the Milanese recordings (LEYDI CH) there are only two. Fortini's speeches are extracted from a larger text, available in typewritten (CRIVELLI) and recorded (IEdM 64/1) versions.

Chapter 12

1   Letter, Michele Straniero to *Musica e dischi*, October 13, 1964, AVANTI Corrvaria 25.

Chapter 13

1   Letter, Gianni Bosio to Vasco Scansani, September 24, 1965, GALLO Corrvaria 27.

2   Bermani (2020: 70–1) suggested that "another song to the tune of 'Bella Ciao'" was sung in the 1930s in the rice fields of Vercelli, and that the version sung by the Maiella Brigade could be "the adaptation of a song from the northern rice fields." The hypothesis, however, remains to be verified.

Chapter 14

1   Domenico Modugno revived "Cade l'uliva" and brought it to national fame in 1972 under the title "Addio addio amore" (Farewell, farewell love); his version is often cited as an adaptation of a traditional tune.

Chapter 15

1   Letter, Michele Straniero to Caterina Bueno, June 10, 1964, AVANTI Corrvaria 25.

2   Letter, Michele Straniero to Giovanna Marini, June 10, 1964, AVANTI Corrvaria 26.

3   Letter, Michele Straniero to Giovanna Daffini, June 10, 1964, AVANTI Corrvaria 25.

4   Letter, Michele Straniero to Mario Lodi, June 10, 1964, AVANTI Corrvaria 26.

Chapter 17

1   I have found no trace of this review. *La Nazione* speaks of a "voce da cortile" (courtyard voice; Griffo 1964), but the term is not intended in a derogatory sense, and the overall review is positive.

2   NCI, *All'Odeon i folksingers del canto di protesta*, press release
(draft), May 1, 1965, NCI 04/5.

Coda

1   Letter, Gruppo Padano di Piadena to Nanni Ricordi, no date
[February 1965], NCI 04/05.

References

Abbiati, F. (1964), "Battibecchi a Spoleto a uno spettacolo di canti popolari," *Il Corriere della Sera*, June 22 [LEYDI MI 71].

Adorno, T.W. ([1938] 2014), "On the Fetish-Character in Music and the Regression of Listening," in J.M. Bernstein (ed.), *The Culture Industry: Selected Essays on Mass Culture*, 29–60, London and New York: Routledge.

Agamennone, M. (2019), *Viaggiando, per onde su onde. Il viaggio di conoscenza, la radiofonia e le tradizioni musicali locali nell'Italia del dopoguerra (1945-1960)*, Rome: Squilibri.

Amadini, F. (1964), "Le canzoni di Spoleto," *La Gazzetta del Popolo*, June 24 [LEYDI MI 71].

Archivio Albanese (2018), *Archivio Guido Albanese 1897–1982*, Ortona: Istituto Nazionale Tostiano. Available online: http://www.istitutonazionaletostiano.it/wp-content/uploads/2018/10/Inventario-Guido-Albanese.pdf (accessed January 25, 2022).

Auslander, P. (2006), "Musical Personae," *The Drama Review*, 50 (1): 100–19.

Barker, H. and Y. Taylor (2007), *Faking It: The Quest for Authenticity in Popular Music*, London: Faber and Faber.

Bermani, C. (1964), "Bella Ciao osteggiata da censura e reazione," *Sesto Città*, June 27 [LEYDI MI 71].

Bermani, C. (1965), "Il repertorio civile di Giovanna Daffini," *Il Nuovo Canzoniere Italiano*, 5: 9–28.

Bermani, C. (1975), liner notes for G. Daffini [33 rpm], *Amore mio non piangere*, I Dischi del Sole DS 1063/65.

Bermani, C. (1978), "Dalla cultura contadina alla cultura urbana," in *Il Nuovo Canzoniere Italiano dal 1962 al 1968*, 5–25, Milan: Gabriele Mazzotta Editore / Istituto Ernesto de Martino.

Bermani, C. (1992), "Giovanna Daffini e Il Nuovo Canzoniere Italiano," in C. Bermani (ed.), *Giovanna Daffini. L'amata genitrice*, 21–46, Gualtieri: Comune di Gualtieri.

Bermani, C. (1997), *Una storia cantata, 1962–1997. Trentacinque anni di attività del Nuovo Canzoniere Italiano-Istituto Ernesto De Martino*, Milan: Jaca Book.

Bermani, C. (2003), "La preistoria del Nuovo Canzoniere Italiano: un colloquio con Roberto Leydi," *il de Martino*, 14: 119–41.

Bermani, C. (2020), *Bella Ciao: storia e fortuna di una canzone. Dalla Resistenza italiana all'universalità delle resistenze*, Novara: Interlinea.

Bertero, G. (1964), "Gorizia fu improvvisata ma dai soldati del 1915–1918," *l'Avanti*, June 24 [LEYDI MI 71].

Bithell, C. and J. Hill, eds. (2014), *The Oxford Handbook of Music Revival*, New York: Oxford University Press.

Bocca, G. (1964), "Tra ballerini e fantasmi 'Bella Ciao' che rivoluzione," *Il Giorno*, June 23 [LEYDI MI 71].

Boffa, G. (1959), "Indonesia: qui si incontrano Asia e Africa," *L'Unità*, November 15.

Bohlman, P.V. (1988), *The Study of Folk Music in the Modern World*, Bloomington: Indiana University Press.

Bohlman, P.V. (1998), [review] "R. Cantwell, *When We Were Good: The Folk Revival*," *American Music*, 16 (1): 91.

Bosio, G. (1964), "Alcune osservazioni sul canto sociale," *Il Nuovo Canzoniere Italiano*, 4: 3–10.

Bosio, G. ([1967] 1998), "Elogio del magnetofono," in *L'intellettuale rovesciato*, 157–66, Milan: Jaca Book.

Bosio, G. and R. Leydi, eds. (1963), *Canti sociali italiani*, Milan: Edizioni del Gallo.

Bosio, G. and R. Leydi ([1965] 2016), [cyclostyle pamphlet], "Bella Ciao e i problemi dell'interpretazione contemporanea delle manifestazioni del mondo popolare," in G. Plastino (ed.), *La musica folk. Storie, protagonisti e documenti del revival in Italia*, 113–19, Milan: il Saggiatore.

Bourdieu, P. (2010), *Distinction: A Social Critique of the Judgement of Taste*, London: Routledge.

Boyes, G. (1993), *The Imagined Village: Culture, Ideology and the English Folk Revival*, Manchester: Manchester University Press.

Bratus, A., M. Corda, F. Guerreschi and F. Maruti (2018), *Il Duo di Piadena: dalle osterie alla televisione*, Cremona: Fantigrafica.

Brecht, B. (1962), *Scritti teatrali*, Turin: Einaudi.

Busetti, F. (1964), "Canti e cantastorie al Festival di Spoleto," *Momento sera*, June 23 [LEYDI MI 71].

Cambria, A. (1964), "Grida e proteste del pubblico a Spoleto," *Stampa Sera*, June 23 [LEYDI MI 71].

Canti della Resistenza italiana (1960), selected by T. Romano and G. Sciolza, with an introduction by Roberto Leydi, Milan: Edizioni del Gallo.

Capriolo, E. (1965), "Storia e controstoria nelle canzoni popolari," *Vie Nuove*, May 13 [NCI 40].

Carpitella, D. (1965), "Il momento umano," *Canzoniere del lavoro*, in *Vie Nuove*, 17, April 29: 31.

Carpitella, D. ([1979] 2016), "La musica e l'etnomusica," *La Biennale di Venezia. Annuario 1978*, 1215–25, Venice: Biennale di Venezia, in G. Plastino (ed.), *La musica folk. Storie, protagonisti e documenti del revival in Italia*, 452–68, Milan: il Saggiatore.

Casiraghi, G. (2005), *Anni settanta. Generazione rock*, Roma: Editori Riuniti.

Chiozzi, M. (1965), "Non ditemi che è bello essere giovani," unknown press [NCI 40].

Ciarpaglini, G. (1964), "Una raccolta di canti popolari," unknown press [LEYDI MI 71].

Cipriani, I. (1964), "Bella ciao, canti dell'altra Italia," *Paese Sera*, June 22 [LEYDI MI 71].

Cirese, A.M. (1953), "Folklore della Resistenza," *La Lapa*, 1 (1): 19–20.

Cirese, A.M. (1973), *Cultura egemonica e culture subalterne*, Palermo: Palumbo.

Coro ARCI (1963), [33 rpm], *Canti partigiani*, a cura di Enzo Lalli, Coro del circolo musicale ARCI "A. Toscanini" di Torino directed by Enrico Lini, DNG GLP 81001.

Crivelli, F. (1963), "Note di un creatore di cabaret," *Sipario*, 212: 40–4, 80.

Crivelli, F. (1964), "La realizzazione di Bella Ciao," *Bella Ciao. Programma di sala*, Festival dei Due Mondi, Spoleto [LEYDI MI 71/02/01].

Daffini, G. (1975), [33 rpm], *Amore mio non piangere*, I Dischi del Sole DS 1063/65.

Daily American (1964), "Army Song Causes Furor at Spoleto," June 25 [LEYDI MI 71].

de Martino, E. (1949), "Intorno a una storia del mondo popolare subalterno," *Società*, 3: 411–35.

de Martino, E. (1952), "Il mondo popolare nel teatro di massa," *Emilia*, 4 (3): 91–3.

Dei, F. (2018), *Cultura popolare in Italia. Da Gramsci all'UNESCO*, 2nd ed., Bologna: Il Mulino.

Deichmann, M. (2016), "Bella Ciao all'Odeon," in G. Plastino (ed.), *La musica folk. Storie, protagonisti e documenti del revival in Italia*, 559–67, Milan: il Saggiatore.

Del Re, G. (1964a), "Arrivano i folksingers," *Il Messaggero*, June 21 [LEYDI MI 71].

Del Re, G. (1964b), "Giusta indignazione per una canzone stonata," *Il Messaggero*, June 22 [LEYDI MI 71].

Eco, U. (1963), "La canzone nuova," *Sipario*, 212: 29–31.

Eco, U. ([1964] 2008), *Apocalittici e integrati*, Milan: Bompiani.

Fabbri, F. (2008), *Around the Clock. Una storia della popular music*, Turin: UTET.

Fabbri, F., G. Plastino and J. Tomatis, "Io lo chiamerei folk music revival. Una conversazione con Giovanna Marini," in G. Plastino (ed.), *La musica folk. Storie, protagonisti e documenti del revival in Italia*, 982–94, Milan: il Saggiatore.

Fanelli, A. (2015), "Il canto sociale come 'folklore contemporaneo' tra demologia, operaismo e storia orale," *Lares*, 81 (2–3): 291–316.

Fanelli, A. (2017), *Contro canto. Le culture della protesta dal canto sociale al rap*, Rome: Donzelli.

Ferraro, D. (2015), *Roberto Leydi e il "Sentite buona gente." Musiche e cultura nel secondo dopoguerra*, Rome: Squilibri.

Flaiano, E. (1964), "La mondina e il cavaliere," *L'Europeo*, June 28 [LEYDI MI 71].

Flores, M. (2020), *Bella Ciao*, Milan: Garzanti.

G.T. (1964), "Molta politica e poca musica," *Il Messaggero*, June 22 [LEYDI MI 71].

Gaber, G. (1965), [45 rpm], "O Bella Ciao / Let's Dance," POP NP 200009.

Gabrielli, G. ([1971] 2016), "La voce dell'altra Italia," *Ciao 2001*, 19: 36–8, in G. Plastino (ed.), *La musica folk. Storie, protagonisti e documenti del revival in Italia*, 622–5, Milan: il Saggiatore.

Galeazzi, L. (2015), [YouTube video], "O Gorizia (tu sei maledetta) Lucilla Galeazzi in Bella Ciao 2015 a Etetrad," Available online: https://www.youtube.com/watch?v=0MmfghNSNIAandab _channel=GaetanoLoPresti (accessed January 25, 2022).

Gelbart, M. (2007), *The Invention of 'Folk Music' and 'Art Music': Emerging Categories from Ossian to Wagner*, Cambridge and New York: Cambridge University Press.

Giacomini, R. (2021), *Bella Ciao. La storia definitiva della canzone partigiana che dalle Marche ha conquistato il mondo*, Rome: Castelvecchi.

Gianelli, M. (1954), "Canzoni e sorrisi di mondine," *Sorrisi e Canzoni*, June 27.

Giannattasio, F. (2011), "Etnomusicologia, 'musica popolare' e folk revival in Italia: il futuro non è più quello di una volta," *AAA TAC, Acoustical Arts and Artifacts. Technology, Aesthetics, Communication*, 8: 65–86.

Giovannetti, A. (1964), "Incidenti al festival di Spoleto durante l'esecuzione di 'Bella Ciao'," *Il Tempo*, June 22 [LEYDI MI 71].

Gobbi, R. (1988), *Il '68 Alla Rovescia*, Il Cammeo, Milan: Longanesi.

Gramsci, A. ([1948] 2011), *Prison Notebooks. Vol. 1*, ed. J.A. Buttigieg, trans. J.A. Buttigieg and A. Callari, New York: Columbia University Press.

Griffo, L. (1964), "Il festival di Spoleto in maniche di camicia," *La Nazione*, June 22 [LEYDI MI 71].

Guizzi, F. (2002), *Guida alla musica popolare in Italia. 3. Gli strumenti*, Lucca: Libreria Musicale Italiana.

Guizzi, F. and I. Meandri (2015), "Velare, svelare. Su alcuni nodi del rapporto tra etnomusicologia e folk revival," in A. Pons (ed.), *Dal folk al pop. La musica occitana fra tradizione e nuovi generi*, 15–36, Torre Pellice: Centro Culturale Valdese Editore.

Harker, D. (1985), *Fakesong. The Manufacture of British 'Folksong' 1700 to the Present Day*, Milton Keynes: Open University Press.

Il Corriere della Sera (1965), "Bella Ciao all'Odeon," May 5 [NCI 40].

Il Messaggero (1964), "Fischi e applausi per Bella ciao a Spoleto," June 27 [LEYDI MI 71].

Ionio, D. (1965), "L'altra Italia in quaranta canzoni," *L'Unità*, May 5 [NCI 40].

L'Espresso (1964), "Contro 'Bella Ciao' scatta il colonnello," June 28 [LEYDI MI 71].

L'Unità (1964), "Interrogazione comunista su 'Bella Ciao'," June 26.

Laing, D. (2014), "MacColl and the English Folk Revival," in A. Moore and G. Vacca (eds.), *Legacies of Ewan MacColl: The Last Interview*, 150–3, Farnham and Burlington, VT: Ashgate.

Leydi, R. (1960), "Osservazioni sulle canzoni della Resistenza italiana nel quadro della nostra musica popolaresca," in *Canti della Resistenza italiana*, selected and annotated by T. Romano and G. Solza, 7–78, Milan: Edizioni del Gallo.

Leydi, R. (1962), "Un canzoniere," *Il Nuovo Canzoniere Italiano*, 1: 2, 5.

Leydi, R. ([1964] 2016), "O chitarra padana," *L'Europeo*, 45 (20): 72–7, in G. Plastino (ed.), *La musica folk. Storie, protagonisti e documenti del revival in Italia*, 550–8, Milan: il Saggiatore.

Leydi, R. (1972), *Il folk music revival*, Palermo: Flaccovio.

Leydi, R. (1992), "Giovanna Daffini e la musica popolare padana," in C. Bermani (ed.), *Giovanna Daffini. L'amata genitrice*, 53–63, Gualtieri: Comune di Gualtieri.

Leydi, R. and T. Kezich (1954), *Ascolta Mr. Bilbo. Canzoni di protesta del popolo americano*, Milan: Edizioni Avanti!.

Livingston, T.E. (1999), "Music Revivals: Towards a General Theory," *Ethnomusicology*, 43 (1): 66.

Lomax, A. (1948), "Foreword," in W. Hille (ed.), *The People's Songbook*, New York: Boni and Gaer.

Lomax, A. (1959a), "Folk Song Style," *American Anthropologist*, 61 (6): 927–54.

Lomax, A. (1959b), "Introduction and Notes on the Songs," in G. Carawan [33 rpm], *Sings—Vol. 2*, Folkways 3548.

Lomax, A. and D. Carpitella, eds. (1957a), [33 rpm] *Northern and Central Italy*, Columbia KL 5173.

Lomax, A. and D. Carpitella, eds. (1957b), [33 rpm] *Southern Italy and the Islands*, Columbia KL 5174.

Longone, R. (1953), "Ragazze di Corea," *L'Unità*, April 29.

Los Marcellos Ferial (1965), [45 rpm] "Lili Marlen / Bella Ciao," Durium CNA9166.

Love, R.E. (2018), Doctoral dissertation, *Songbook for a Revolution. Popular Culture and the New Left in 1960s Italy*, New York University, Department of Italian Studies [IEdM].

Love, R.E. (2019), "Talking Italian Blues: Roberto Leydi, Giovanna Marini and American Influence in the Italian Folk Revival, 1954–1966," *Popular Music*, 38 (2): 317–34.

Macchiarella, I. (2005), *Il canto necessario. Giovanna Marini compositrice, didatta e interprete*, Udine: Nota.

Malagugini, S. and C. Mattea (2016), "Spoleto, 1964," in G. Plastino (ed.), *La musica folk. Storie, protagonisti e documenti del revival in Italia*, 523–8, Milan: il Saggiatore.

Mantovani, S. (1966), "I modi interpretativi del canto popolare," in *Strumenti di lavoro 1: Comunicazioni di massa e comunicazioni di classe*, 176–91, Milan: Edizioni del Gallo.

Mantovani, S. ([1972] 2016), "I modi interpretativi del canto popolare (1965–1970)," in R. Leydi, *Il folk music revival*, 233–46, Palermo: Flaccovio, in G. Plastino (ed.), *La musica folk. Storie, protagonisti e documenti del revival in Italia*, 236–47, Milan: il Saggiatore.

Marini, G. (1992), "L'imposto di Giovanna Daffini," in C. Bermani (ed.), *Giovanna Daffini. L'amata genitrice*, 81–3, Gualtieri: Comune di Gualtieri.

Marini, G. (2005), *Una mattina mi son svegliata. La musica e le storie di un'Italia perduta*, Milan: Rizzoli.

Marini, G. (2012), "Col senno del poi," in G. Morandi, *Spoleto 1964. Bella Ciao: il diario*, 9–13, Sesto Fiorentino: il de Martino.

Milva (1965), [45 rpm], "Bella Ciao / Non mi va," Cetra SP 1283.

Miranda, C. (1964), "Ricacciate in gola ai sovversivi le canzoni che offendono l'Italia," *Secolo XX*, July 7 [LEYDI MI 71].

Montand, Y. (1962), [45 rpm], *Canta in italiano* [France], *Souvenir italiano* [Italy], Philips 432 735 BE.

Moore, A. (2002), "Authenticity as Authentication," *Popular Music*, 21 (2): 209–23.

Moore, A. and G. Vacca, eds. (2014), *Legacies of Ewan MacColl: The Last Interview*, Farnham and Burlington, VT: Ashgate.

Morandi, G. ([1965] 2012), *Spoleto 1964. Bella Ciao: il diario*, Sesto Fiorentino: il de Martino.

NCI (1964), *Bella Ciao. Programma di sala*, Festival dei Due Mondi, Spoleto [LEYDI MI 71/02/01].

NCI (1965a), [33 rpm] *Le canzoni di Bella Ciao*, I Dischi del Sole DS 101/3.

NCI (1965b), *Bella Ciao. Programma di sala*, Teatro Odeon, Milan [NCI].

NCI (1965c) [video footage], Fragments from the Milan shows, 8mm film [IEdM]. Available online: https://archive.org/details/BellaCiaoRedux.

NCI (1966), *Strumenti di lavoro 3: Discussioni di temi e decisioni organizzative; Milano, Ottobre–Dicembre 1965*, Milan: Edizioni del Gallo.

NCI (1975), [33 rpm] *Italie / Bella Ciao—Chansons du Peuple en Italie*, Harmonia Mundi HMU 734.

NCI (1992), [CD], *Le canzoni di Bella Ciao*, Bravø Records BR128553735–2.

Nenni, P. (1960), [45 rpm], *Appello elettorale*, I Dischi del Sole DS 1.

Neri, V. (1964), "Andrà in carcere per una canzone?," *TV Sorrisi e canzoni*, July 5.

Nigra, C. ([1888] 2009), *Canti popolari del Piemonte*, eds. F. Castelli, E. Jona and A. Lovatto, Turin: Einaudi.

Nilsson, M. (1963?), [45 rpm], *Dansa Twist*, Philips 433 417 PE.

Ong, W.J. (1982), *Orality and Literacy: The Technologizing of the Word*, London: Methuen.

Ord, M. (2017), Doctoral dissertation, *Sound Recording in the British Folk Revival: Ideology, Discourse and Practice, 1950–1975*, Newcastle University, International Centre for Music Studies.

Ortoleva, P. (1998), *I movimenti del '68 in Europa e in America*, 2nd ed., Rome: Editori Riuniti.

Pestelli, C. (2014), "An Escape from Escapism: The Short History of Cantacronache," in F. Fabbri and G. Plastino (eds.), *Made in Italy. Studies in Italian Popular Music*, 153–61, London and New York: Routledge.

Pestelli, C. (2016), *Bella Ciao. La canzone della libertà*, Turin: Add.

Pietrangeli, P. (1968), [45 rpm] "Risoluzione dei Comunardi—Il vestito di Rossini / Contessa," I Dischi del Sole LR 45/11.

Plastino, G. (2016), "Introduzione," in G. Plastino (ed.), *La musica folk. Storie, protagonisti e documenti del revival in Italia*, 17–58, Milan: il Saggiatore.

Provantini, A. (1964), "Questa commedia non s'ha da fare," *Vie Nuove*, July 30 [LEYDI MI 71].

R.B. (1965), "Si può cantare anche senza odio," *Oggi illustrato*, May 20 [LEYDI MI 71].

Ratushniak, L. (1964), "Zapreshennaja pesnya," *Sovetskaya Kultura*, June 21 [LEYDI MI 71].

Ravaioli, C. (1964), "Invitano in salotto le canzoni di osteria," *Settimana INCOM*, July 26, 30–3.

Ricci, R. (1947), "Giovani di tutto il mondo sfilano allo stadio di Praga," *L'Unità*, June 27.

Ronström, O. (1996), "Revival Reconsidered," *The World of Music*, 38 (3): 5–20.

Ruschetto, G. (1965), "Music Capitals of the World—Milan," *Billboard*, August 21, 25.

Sala, E. (2015), "Canzone 'nuova' e identità milanese al Teatro Gerolamo (1958–1963)," *Musica/Realtà*, 107: 63–76.

Sanzò, D. (1964), "Claque rossa in visone," *Lo Specchio*, July 5 [LEYDI 71].

Sassu, P. (2011), "Dall'etnofonia all'etnomusicologia. Un secolo di studi sulla musica popolare italiana," *Archivio di etnografia*, 6 (1–2): 37–68.

Scotti, M. (2018), *Vita di Giovanni Pirelli. Tra cultura e impegno militante*, Rome: Donzelli.

Settimelli, L. (1964a), "I canti popolari arrivano a Spoleto," *L'Unità*, June 12 [LEYDI MI 71].

Settimelli, L. (1964b), "*Bella Ciao* spettacolo vigoroso e avvincente," *L'Unità*, June 22 [LEYDI MI 71/4-5-6].

Simeone, W.E. (1959), [review] "A. Lomax, D. Carpitella, *Northern and Central Italy; Southern Italy and the Islands*," *The Journal of American Folklore*, 72 (283): 90.

Straniero, G. and M. Barletta (2003), *La rivolta in musica. Michele L. Straniero e il Cantacronache nella storia della musica italiana*, Turin: Lindau.

Straniero, M.L. (1965), "*Bella Ciao* a Spoleto," *Il Nuovo Canzoniere Italiano*, 5: 62–7.

Straniero, M.L. (1971), "La canzone di protesta in Italia," in R.-U. Kaiser (ed.), *Guida alla musica pop*, 276–86, Milan: Mondadori.

Straniero, M.L. and S. Liberovici (1958), "Perché il disco EP 45 CS," *Cantacronache*, 1: 9–10, Edizioni Italia Canta.

Straniero, M.L., S. Liberovici, E. Jona and G. De Maria (1964), *Le canzoni della cattiva coscienza*, Milan: Bompiani.

Tesi, R., L. Galeazzi, E. Ledda, G. Di Marco, A. Salvadori and G. Biolcati (2015), [CD], *Bella Ciao*, Visage VM3008.

The Minstrels (1965), [45 rpm] "Bella Ciao / The Drinkin' Gourd," CBS 1349.

Tomatis, J. (2014), "A Portrait of the Author as an Artist. Cantautori and Canzone d'autore: Ideology, Authenticity, Stylization," in F. Fabbri and G. Plastino (eds.), *Made in Italy. Studies in Italian Popular Music*, 87–99, London and New York: Routledge.

Tomatis, J. (2016a), "Il Folk Festival di Torino, 1965–1966," in G. Plastino (ed.), *La musica folk. Storie, protagonisti e documenti del revival in Italia*, 122–43, Milan: il Saggiatore.

Tomatis, J. (2016b), "La 'nuova canzone' e il folk revival. Narrazioni, intrecci e scontri di generi musicali fra anni sessanta e settanta," in G. Plastino (ed.), *La musica folk. Storie, protagonisti e documenti del revival in Italia*, 1059–82, Milan: il Saggiatore.

Tomatis, J. (2019), *Storia culturale della canzone italiana*, Milan: Il Saggiatore.

Tomatis, J. (2021), "I due Gramsci. Per una archeologia del 'popolare' musicale in Italia," *La Valle dell'Eden*, 37: 84–98.

Turino, T. (2008), *Music as Social Life: The Politics of Participation*, Chicago: University of Chicago Press.

V.B. (1965), "Spirituals in risaia," *Avanti!*, May 5 [NCI 40].

Valtorta, L. (2018), "Giovanna Marini: 'Vi racconto il mio 68'," *La Repubblica*, February 6. Available online: https://www.repubblica.it/spettacoli/musica/2018/02/06/news/giovanna_marini-188104057/ (accessed January 25, 2022).

Various (1960), [33 rpm EP] *Canti di protesta del popolo italiano 2*, eds. Sergio Liberovici and Emilio Jona, Italia Canta SP33 R/ 0013.

Various (1961), [33 rpm] *Canti della Resistenza spagnola 1939/1961*, Italia Canta MP 33/CRA/0026.

Various (1962), [33 rpm EP] *Canti del lavoro*, I Dischi del Sole DS 4.

Various (1963), [33 rpm EP] *Canti della Resistenza italiana 2*, I Dischi del Sole DS 8.

Various (1966), [33 rpm EP] *I canti del lavoro 4*, I Dischi del Sole DS 37.

Vie Nuove (1964), "I folksingers dei due mondi," June 18 [LEYDI MI 71].

Zak, A. III. (2012), "No-Fi: Crafting a Language of Recorded Music in 1950s Pop," in S. Frith and S. Zagorski-Thomas (eds.), *The Art of Record Production: An Introductory Reader for a New Academic Field*, 43–56, Farnham: Ashgate.

Index

Index